CHILDREN'S LITERATURE IN THE CURRICULUM

# Children's Literature in the Curriculum

*by Dewey W. Chambers*

UNIVERSITY OF THE PACIFIC

RAND McNALLY & COMPANY  ·  CHICAGO

RAND McNALLY EDUCATION SERIES

B. Othanel Smith, *Advisory Editor*

CARTREFLE COLLEGE OF EDUCATION
WREXHAM

# TABLE OF CONTENTS

INTRODUCTION, *page ix*

*Section One:* *The Role of Literature in
the Elementary Curriculum*                                    1

*Chapter I*  CHILDREN'S LITERATURE AND
THE READING PROGRAM                                           3

The Traditional Role                                          6
Reading Growth and Children's Literature                     10
The Basal Approach                                           15
The Individualized Reading Program                           19
The Best of Both                                             23
Literature and the Remedial Reader                           25
Controlled Vocabulary                                        29
Summary                                                      30
Exercises for the Teacher                                    33
Suggested Readings                                           35

*Chapter II*  CHILDREN'S LITERATURE  AND
THE SOCIAL STUDIES                                           37

Depth of Understanding                                       40
The Emotional Dimension                                      44
The Informational Book                                       46

*v*

Social Studies Activities     51
The Biography     55
Human Relations     60
Summary     65
Exercises for the Teacher     68
Suggested Readings     70

Chapter III    CHILDREN'S LITERATURE AND THE SCIENCES     72

The Elementary Science Program     74
Reading and the Science Program     76
The Trade Book in the Science Program     77
New Approaches in Science Education     78
Extending and Deepening Concepts Beyond the Textbook     81
Keeping Abreast of New Developments in Science     86
Enrichment     88
The Science Activity     91
Cross-Reference Checking     93
The Science Hobby     94
Summary     99
Exercises for the Teacher     101
Suggested Readings     103

Chapter IV    CHILDREN'S LITERATURE AND THE ARTS     104

Exposing Children to the Best Writing in Our Language     106
Developing Taste in Children's Literature     109
The Art of Illustration     114
Initial Introduction to Poetry     119
The Art of the Playwright     122
Children's Literature and Creative Drama     123
The Arts and Nonfiction Literature for Children     127
Folk Literature, Our Literary Heritage     128

Summary                                                     130
Exercises for the Teacher                                   132
Suggested Readings                                          133


*Section Two:   How Books Can Affect Children*             135


*Chapter V*  THE DIDACTIC THEORY                           137

How Books Affect Children                         140
Research on the Effects of Books on Children      142
Research on the Content of Children's Literature  150
Bibliotherapy                                     158
Exercises for the Teacher                         163
Suggested Readings                                164


*Chapter VI*  CHILDREN'S LITERATURE AND
             CREATIVE THINKING                             165

Children's Literature and the Stimulation
    of Divergent Thinking                         167
Children's Literature as a Springboard for
    Creative Activity                             170
Summary                                           175
Exercises for the Teacher                         176
Suggested Readings                                177


*Section Three:   Thoughts on Some Controversial Issues
                 in Children's Literature*                 179


*Chapter VII*  SPECIAL ISSUES IN
              CHILDREN'S LITERATURE                        181

The Modern "Chapbook"                          182
The Book Report                                186
The Award Winners                              191
The Classics                                   200

| | |
|---|---|
| The Paperback | 205 |
| The Series Books | 208 |
| The Controlled Vocabulary | 212 |

BIBLIOGRAPHY, *page 215*

INDEX, *page 223*

# INTRODUCTION

*Quite frankly, this book is a plea !*
Some may call it a rationale, but the author's intent was to plead the case of children's literature as an integral part of the elementary school's curriculum, as well as an important factor in the lives of children. Perhaps a word somewhere in between *plea* and *rationale* would best describe this work. Unfortunately our language does not provide for such an idea. More's the pity !

The wonderful world of children's books has delighted millions of fortunate children for many years. That, by and large, is what books are supposed to do ! Aside from some of the early didactic writing wherein morals and manners were hammered home via the printed page, the literature that is written for children is among the most treasured and enjoyed in our culture. From early childhood to adolescence, that special genre of literature prevails.

In this book, children's literature will be broadly defined as any creative literary work that has been especially written and designed for children's use. That literature, by and large, is meant to play three major roles. It is meant to delight, to inform and to affect the values and understandings of its young readers. First and most importantly, however, it is meant to delight. Children's literature is an aesthetic experience for the young provided through the medium of ink on paper. In the context of this book, children's literature will include fiction, folk tales, the classics, informational books, poetry, biographies . . . and the like. While this spectrum is broad, it will not include the realm of the textbook. For the reader of this book, a clear dichotomy must exist between that which is a textbook and the broad definition of children's literature offered here. Perhaps the thumbnail definition of the difference between text and trade book given by Professor

Shelton Root Jr. of the University of Georgia says it best. "The text-book is to be used *on* children. The trade book is to be used *by* children. We are concerned with the latter." And so are we.

The world of children's literature is indeed a special one. It has demanded, and does demand, attention for itself alone. The attention that children's literature has recently received, as a literary form, is superb ! The outstanding works by Arbuthnot, Huck, Young, Hazard, Smith, *et al.* attest to this scholarly attention. The student or devotee of children's literature has a wealth of excellent material available to him.

The book that this section introduces in no way attempts to replace or compete with those fine works concerned with the literary aspect of literature for children. In fact, the author suggests that one of the many fine books that discuss the general nature of children's literature accompany, or precede, this one. It is hoped that the present book, and those that deal with the intrinsic literary quality of children's books, will reinforce each other.

*Children's Literature in the Curriculum* is a pragmatic look at the role good children's books can play in the curriculum of our elementary schools, the effect they may have on the developing person, and a discussion of several important issues concerning children and their literature. This book is written for and geared toward the needs of the practicing elementary teacher, the consultant in elementary education, and the student of elementary education. It is a curriculum-oriented book with literature for children as its central theme. It is an attempt to help teachers recognize the part that literature for children can play in developing a dynamic, meaningful curriculum for today's children.

In a book of this nature, where the author attempts to convince the reader of the important role literature can play in the curriculum and in the lives of children, the temptation to compile a book list for each special role is a strong one. Regardless of how strong that temptation is, however, the task would be presumptive, redundant, and monumental. The mere facts that over three thousand new children's titles are published each year (along with the reissuing of older and successful titles, plus the classics), that there are excellent existing book lists available in each area, and that teachers need, and want, firsthand knowledge of the books they will use, make that temptation less than useful, if not somewhat silly ! Despite the author's personal objection to this strong temptation, some books are recommended, and a complete list of aids, booklists and other writings are included in each chapter and in the appendix of this book. Presumptive, redundant, and monumental or not, specific suggestions are made. However, the recipe syndrome, found so often in texts of this nature, has been, hopefully, avoided.

In writing this book the author, an elementary teacher himself for ten years, attempted to bring theory into a practical framework. He attempted to offer models and examples that could serve the teacher in a useful, practical way. Theory is the foundation of any successful teaching practice. Theory, by itself, however, often remains at a lofty level—not translated into the practical, workable tools that the teacher needs when she practices the art of teaching. The contents of this book have attempted to bring theory and practical application into close juxtaposition. While in no way seeking to be "an educational recipe book," the contents do seek to be of practical value based upon sound learning and curriculum theory.

*Children's Literature in the Curriculum* is a departure from the usual concept of books about children's literature. It is intended to be so ! The author knows the fine works that exist in that realm, and is not so foolish as to attempt an improvement. What he has done is to offer new ideas about the use of that literature in the lives of the children for whom it was written.

It is, quite frankly, a plea !

*SECTION ONE*

# The Role of Literature
# in the Elementary Curriculum

*Chapter I*

# CHILDREN'S LITERATURE
# AND THE READING PROGRAM

*One of the most important,*
and certainly one of the most stressed, tasks of the elementary
school is to help children learn to read. This job of learning to
read starts early in the youngster's school career and continues
for many years. Fortunately for most children, it is a task that is
successfully completed. For others, it is not. The job of learning
to read is a difficult and complex one. The casualty in this process
is, indeed, unfortunate.

The teacher approaches her role in this task with respect,
sincerity, and skill. She has been professionally educated by the
college or university so that she can help the youngster unravel
the mysteries of the printed page. She employs all the professional
knowledge at her command. For many teachers the task of helping
the child learn to read is the most important task of the day. The
conscientious reading teacher will often slight other curricular
areas so that more time and attention can be devoted to the teaching of reading. "What can they do in school if they can't read?"
teachers ask. The question is a moot one. The American school
*is* a reading school, and the ability to read is a prerequisite for
success in it.

The parent, so eager for his child to succeed, watches his youngster's growth in reading with interest and sometimes alarm. He, too, knows the importance of the reading skills. He is pleased when his youngster recognizes the symbols on the printed page and is able to call them by name. He is a proud parent, indeed, when he hears his child read from the text and derive meaning from the print. His frustration and disappointment, however, are very real and very immediate if his youngster is less than successful in his attempts to learn to read. His concern for his youngster's success in school often hinges upon that youngster's success with reading skills. Many parents are convinced that failure in school comes as a direct result of poor reading ability. They are often correct in that assumption.

The concern that parents as well as educators have about the teaching of reading has resulted in a mass of data, materials, and information about how to help children learn to read. So earnest is this concern that methods of teaching to read have developed with something akin to a philosophy. Organizations have emerged that stress a point of view, a method, or a particular philosophy concerning the teaching of reading. Extensive and scholarly research has investigated most aspects of how children learn to read; the best method of teaching reading; problems youngsters and teachers face when they meet to achieve the task of learning to read; print size, book format, content, vocabulary, and the like. This research continues and will probably continue for years to come. The result of this research is of unquestioned value. Professional educators know more about the teaching of reading than almost any other area in the curriculum as a result of this work.

Critics of education, some sincere and some sensational, have jumped into the fray. A wealth of books and articles questioning Johnny's ability to read have appeared in book stores, on newsstands, and in the popular press. These critics have asked questions about reading instruction and in some cases have given answers about it too. Podia across the country resound with verbal thrusts and parries over Johnny and his battle with the printed word. Bridge clubs and coffee klatches find the "reading program" a favorite discussion topic. The method of how reading should be taught has taken on an almost emotional aura. Camps have been formed and lines drawn as to how Johnny is to be taught to read.

The first question at parent-teacher conference time is likely to be concerned with the child's growth in reading. The first mark on a report card to attract a parent's attention is probably that mark which evaluates the youngster's reading progress. The concern is real and valid.

Textbook companies, sensing the concern of parents and teachers with the reading program, have produced a multitude of materials that are designed to help teachers successfully relate reading skills to the pupils. Entire reading programs, handsomely designed and based for the most part on sound educational principles are available to teachers. New approaches to the teaching of reading, some good and some completely ridiculous, appear regularly under the banner of eager publishing firms. Textbook companies are enjoying an undreamed of period of eminence. Some actually promise a panacea. Several reading series present teaching as an automatic "foolproof" task, in that the teacher's manual is so specific that it forbids any real, imaginative teaching. "Just follow the manual," they tell us, "and reading skills will result." Unfortunately, there are those that, by persuasion or necessity, believe in this kind of teaching.

Textbook companies are constantly searching for new and better ways of helping teachers teach reading. If a better way is found, they rightfully believe, the text series or the approach that offers it will be financially successful.

It is sometimes confusing for a conscientious reading teacher to know which direction to move in the teaching of reading. The programs that are offered all promise certain results, and most of them deliver. Is the basal reading program best? What about ITA? The color-coded reading cards offer certain advantages. The programed approach? Many attest to the experience method. And so it goes—what's best, and for whom? What shall the teacher use to best help the youngster acquire the skills of reading?

The concern that both professional educators and parents have about teaching children to read has indeed had fine results. The reading teacher is in an enviable position when she can wonder about the best approach and have ample research to help her decide. She is fortunate to have publishers vying for her attention with the beautifully produced materials that they have had designed. Parental concern certainly undergirds her work at school in helping the child learn to read. University and college class-rooms offer her the newest and best ways to work with the youngster in gaining control of reading skills. A wealth of material is at her beck and call in helping Johnny learn to read.

This concern has resulted in a strong emphasis on the teaching of reading in classrooms across the country. Teachers and administrators, that conscientious group, have determined that Johnny's younger brother and sister will read with more skill and facility than Johnny did. Concentration on the teaching of reading in the elementary classrooms is making sure that this effort will bring about these results. It has been suggested, however, that perhaps these efforts are more of a hindrance than an aid in helping Johnny's younger brother and sister to learn to read. Perhaps we are doing too much teaching. Perhaps our conscientious efforts have resulted in over-teaching. *Perhaps, along with teaching children to read, we should let them read, as well.*

The ultimate reason for the teaching of reading is to introduce the world of books to the student. We hope that as a result of our teaching, students will use the reading skills as tools to utilize fully the wonder of the printed word. We mean, in short, to teach reading so that students will read—not to teach reading just for the sake of teaching to read.

The use of the basal reader or other devices designed to aid the teacher in the area of skill development is a generally accepted practice. These aids in the teaching of reading have been so developed that sequence of skills, vocabulary, eye sweep, print size, etc. have been carefully and, in most cases, well organized. They do, by and large, what they claim to do: help the teacher develop reading skills. But that is all they do. Certainly, a good reading program needs to do more than develop skills. What about putting these skills to use? *Why not let the students read, once we have taught them how?*

## THE TRADITIONAL ROLE

If, indeed, the purpose of teaching reading is to open up the world of books to students, to give them skills so that they can unlock words and react to ideas in print, to help them know that the skills we teach them have value, then how have we traditionally gone about this task?

Often one needs only to remember the classrooms that he himself was a part of as a child. Unfortunately, we sometimes need only to look at our own classrooms or the classrooms of our colleagues to see the traditional role of literature in the reading program. We see, too often, that teachers are so busy helping children develop skills that they neglect the important aspects of helping children understand how to use these skills. It is sometimes true, unfortunately, that we do teach reading for reading alone. We sometimes become so involved with the task of teaching that we forget its purpose!

The delightful world of children's literature should be an integral part of every good reading program. Thousands of children's trade books available in an ever-increasing range of interest, subject, and ability levels are a ready source for teachers. Yet, in many classrooms, how is this treasury of materials used? How does the student come in contact with literature for children, that delightful treasure trove that lets him use and practice his reading skills? To what position is children's literature relegated in the reading program—or the classroom, for that matter—in the traditional curriculum?

Too often literature for children is used as a "free time" activity, to be enjoyed "after all the work has been done." The youngster may have a book in his desk that can be brought out when the text material has been completed, the workbook has been satisfied, and he has nothing else to do that is of "value." The teacher in a classroom of this sort sees the trade book as a way of keeping the youngster occupied and out of trouble—as a filler between assignments. This attitude, of course, relegates reading, *real* reading, to the area of "not important" in the child's thinking. The collection of trade books languishes in the corner and, if used, is approached in a haphazard way. Children are, whether we like it or not, *taught by the attitude that books are not important and that the enjoyment of reading is secondary to the practice of endless skills and completion of a number of workbook pages.* The idea that the skills of reading are a gift that can open wonderful and magical doors to a world of literature is often left to go begging!

In too many traditional elementary classrooms a visit to the school or community library is considered an "extracurricular" activity, and is treated as such. In some classrooms, a library visit is actually considered an after-school activity. The teaching program must not be disrupted for learning!

Instead of this attitude, children should expect regular library visits as part of the ongoing educational program. These visits should be exciting, fruitful times of adventure and exploration. It is here that the student and teacher can browse, hunt, share, and become genuinely excited about the prospects of what a book holds in store. It is in the library that we can help children realize that the reading skills we work so hard to develop have real use.

When the library visit ends, and the group returns to the classroom with choices in hand, let them read. Capitalize on their fresh excitement, their curiosity of what is in the books they have chosen. The motivation we seek to develop for a good lesson in other curricular areas is obviously apparent in a situation of this kind.

Bill cannot wait to find out about the Indian battle so colorfully illustrated in his book. Alice's book about cats will answer many of the questions she has about the care and feeding of kittens, now that she has one. Tom, a Tod Moran fan, has found another exciting Howard Pease book and is anxious to be off on another rousing adventure at sea. John, a slow reader and somewhat immature for his age, has chosen another picture storybook. He can read the pictures better than he can the words, at this point, and gets much satisfaction from doing so. This is the time for children to find the wonder of the printed page, the beauty of language and illustration. It is at this time that they need to be surrounded by the wonderful world of children's literature using the skills of reading we have given them. A period of half an hour to forty-five minutes spent in reading, at this time, is a good educational investment.

Of course, there are those who will say that recreational reading, or reading for pleasure, should go on, in large part, outside of school time. We are told the day should be for instructional purposes; a time to teach. The writer quite agrees! Classroom time *is* a time to teach. And good teaching can go on when youngsters have returned from the library eager and willing to explore the books they have chosen. What good teaching it is to let children learn. How fine it is to let children learn that reading skills do open doors to wonderful adventures and provide answers to youthful questions. What a wonderful experience it is to learn to appreciate a book for what it is and for what it can do. Expert teaching can provide a situation in which youngsters can acquire positive attitudes toward the printed page which will turn them into readers, not youngsters who know just how to read.

Of course, books should go home, too. We should encourage children to take books home for enjoyment. We want our youngsters to know that what they do in school has relevance to their life out of school. The reading adventure started during class time sometimes cannot wait to be continued tomorrow; it must be continued after school, or that night. The valuable information about how to keep turtles needs to go home and be shared with other family members. The picture book is just too good to be left at school; it needs to go home and be enjoyed again and again. The good book, the book the child has found and wants, will go home.

As teachers, however, we know that we cannot always depend upon the home as a place that is conducive to reading. We must remember that the classroom is, for many children, the only quiet, orderly place in their lives. For many children, the classroom is the only place they can read and enjoy reading. Many homes are busy places complete with television set, radio, younger children, and the ordinary bustle of household activities. Often the child and his book cannot compete with this activity. Some homes, of course, simply do not have the facilities, either emotional or physical, to be a place where reading can happen. In some cases youngsters must share in household tasks and after the evening meal physical exhaustion often stops them from reading. Some children who need physical activity after school will choose the playground, the skating rink, the basketball court, or the swimming pool. Reading, of course, has its place; it will not, however, replace needed physical activity, sleep, or family life. For many children, then, the only place they can read is in the classroom. How sad it is when we cannot provide that opportunity. How unfortunate it is that we are so busy teaching that we cannot provide opportunities for our students to learn. It is really a conscientiously misguided effort when we, as reading teachers, concern ourselves with just the teaching of skills and neglect to help our students see that these skills have use and wonderful possibilities of application.

## READING GROWTH
## AND CHILDREN'S LITERATURE

Is the teacher who places children's literature in the role of an extracurricular activity to be read out of school or when all "valuable" work has been completed in the classroom, a teacher who is not concerned about the education of children? Probably not. This teacher is likely to be one who is very concerned about making every moment count in the classroom. This teacher probably believes that the skills must be taught and that the reading program in the elementary school is where those skills must be learned. She is probably very conscientious and is likely to examine reading scores with both interest and alarm. She is convinced that skill development must be the major concern in the elementary reading program, for after all, "they can't read those books without the skills." Reading can come later, she thinks, after the skills are firm. Her desire to teach children the skills of reading is sincere. Her philosophy about reading is likewise sincere. She wants to do the best job of teaching reading that she can. Her motivation is honest.

Every thinking educator must agree that the skills of reading are a necessary part of the reading program. One cannot learn to read by just picking up a book and looking at it. Skills and controls must be developed if the mysteries of the printed page are to be understood and print is to be of use. The teaching of reading means just that: reading skills must be taught. A good, developmental, sequential program is a necessity if we hope to help youngsters learn to read.

The role that children's literature plays in the acquisition of, and readiness for, reading skills, as well as the opportunity to exercise those skills, is often not known in sufficient depth by teachers. The teacher education courses at colleges and universities, by necessity, concentrate on helping prospective teachers learn to teach the skills of reading in the developmental way. Discussions and lectures usually point out the value of a good recreational reading program and the topics then go on to other and necessary aspects of how to teach reading developmentally. A one-semester or one-quarter course in the highly complex job of teaching reading and the language arts often leaves much to be desired in the education of a professional teacher.

University courses in children's literature, when they are offered, usually concern themselves with book content, author style, kinds of children's literature available, and material of this nature. Seldom can a professor of children's literature afford the time to discuss reading methodology and the role, technique-wise, of literature in the task of developmental reading. Yet, professional literature reports on studies that have proven the value of children's literature in the reading program.* These studies, done at some of our finest universities under the guidance of the best reading authorities in the nation, have given us real evidence that children's literature does play an important role in the development of skills and attitudes of reading. These studies have investigated reading and language development from preschool level and Head Start projects to primary grade levels, intermediate grade levels, and upward. They have shown that the role of children's literature is a significant factor in a good reading program. The studies have also shown us time and again that the basal program, or the pure developmental reading program, is a limiting factor in helping children to learn to read.

The implications of these studies have produced a wealth of journal articles and books which discuss the role children's literature can and should play in a good reading program. These articles and books should be a significant factor in easing a teacher's mind about bringing children and books together in a classroom setting. They clearly show that skill development and test scores are higher when the developmental reading program provides children with the opportunity to read for recreation and information through trade books.

---

* See the suggested readings at the end of this chapter.

It seems evident then that the conscientious reading teacher would rush to the library and gather an interesting and varied collection of trade books for use in her classroom. It seems obvious too that if teachers desire to improve the reading programs that now exist, they would investigate the reading methods or plans that have been developed so that they can include children's trade books as a regular part of the reading program. It would seem that school budgets would provide a healthy portion for the acquisition of children's trade books as necessary instructional tools, in light of the research that tells us the value of children's literature in the reading program. Perhaps this will happen! There seem to be movements in that direction. One would hope that, as educators, we do not ignore the truth as revealed through scientific study. One would hope that we do not remain traditional in our schools for the sake of tradition but move forward to better ways with the new knowledge we have.

What has research told us about the role of children's literature in reading skill development? It would take many tomes to relate it all. For our purposes, however, it may be good to list some generalizations concerning skill and attitude development that have come about as a result of research. The conscientious reading teacher will want to know that:

1. Preschool language (vocabulary) development is increased significantly if children are provided a rich experience through children's books. Oral reading to young children and much interaction with picture storybooks are advised.

2. In working with disadvantaged children (in projects such as Head Start, as well as in the classroom), the opportunity to interact with children's books increases language development and thus increases their ability to successfully cope with beginning reading instruction.

3. The relationship between oral language and reading has been confirmed. Oral language can be enlarged and significantly enhanced by interaction with children's books when read aloud.

4. The slower the youngster is in his academic progress (reading), the more difficult it is for him to deal with words

The real reason for the teaching of reading in our schools is to produce readers of books, not children who just know how to read. The gift of reading and the opportunity to use that gift is a sacred trust of all teachers.

A wealth of good children's literature needs to be available
to all children as they attempt to learn the skills of reading.
We hope children will learn more than just how to read.
We hope they will be encouraged to read as they are learning.

*School setting: Lincoln Elementary School, Stockton, California*
PHOTO: APERTURE LIMITED, STOCKTON, CALIFORNIA

in isolation, unrelated to a meaningful experience. Vocabulary is thus learned best in a context of emotional and intellectual meaning. The children's trade book is a good source for this kind of learning.

5. The advanced reader is better able to achieve greater growth when children's books are a part of his reading program than he may achieve from a basal program alone.

6. Because of the emotional involvement that occurs when a youngster reads a book of his choice, his use of context skills often overcomes what appears to be problems in other reading situations.

7. Because more reading is done when children's books are a part of the reading program, skills are given an opportunity to be used more often. They thus are more likely to become a part of the child's collection of permanent reading tools.

8. Because boredom is less likely to occur when a rich program of literature is evident in a reading program, attitudes toward learning to read improve significantly.

9. Research does not indicate that children learn to read best by the traditional basal reading approach. Evidence is present to indicate the opposite to be true.*

10. The youngster who has failed to respond to traditional approaches in reading instruction often responds to an approach based upon the individualization of his instruction using trade books rather than textbooks as instructional material.

## THE BASAL APPROACH

Do the preceding comments indicate that there is no place for the basal reading program or other developmental instructional devices in the teaching of reading? Shall we negate the traditional approach altogether? One hopes not! There is a place for the traditional reading program in our elementary schools, and it has an important place, too. To ignore the fine work that has been done

---

* See suggested readings at the end of this chapter.

in helping us teach reading through the medium of the basal reader, or other developmental devices, would, indeed, be foolish.

The basal reading program has many strengths. It is usually a well-planned, sequential program, based upon expert advice and research on how to help children unlock words so that meaning can result. The basal reader works to develop phonetic and structural analysis, skills that are aids in helping children understand the code of print. Real effort is placed on helping children comprehend what they read in the text. The text often suggests creative activity that takes the youngster beyond the word-recognition stage and attempts to place him in the role of an interpreter. We cannot deny it—the basal program is usually a carefully thought out, well-planned approach to help children develop the skills of reading.

The basal program comes to us in many forms. We have the ITA, the Linguistic Approach, SRA, and Sullivan, as well as the many traditional reading programs from various publishers. Some publishers are producing material that is geared to certain cultural and ethnic groups in our society in the hope that these groups of children will identify with it and thus acquire reading skills. A great deal of thought and effort have been spent in producing these basal plans. To ignore their effectiveness in certain skill areas would be folly.

Teachers also like the security of using these basal reading programs. They offer lesson plans, a sequence of skill development that leaves little to chance, and a sense of professional well-being in that the organization of these programs is really a wonder of modern education. Many teachers, especially new, inexperienced ones, recall the training they received in their professional education. Many of them used the basal materials as they learned some of the techniques of teaching reading. These materials are familiar to the new teacher as she starts her professional work with youngsters. As familiar tools in the untried seas of teaching, they are something upon which she can count. This is evident when one supervises student teachers in their first attempts at teaching. Should the dormitory or sorority house ever catch on fire, the teacher's guide for the basal reading series would precede most personal material out the window to safety.

The basal programs do, indeed, have strengths. They have

weaknesses, too. They are not the panacea that many think they are. They do not do a complete job of teaching reading and, in some cases, actually hinder the reading program. They can be considered dangerous, if they are accepted *carte blanche*, to do the whole job.

The basal program is often organized around clusters of children reading at various levels. The program usually finds a group reading above grade level, at grade level, and below grade level. Each of these clusters of children is taught as a separate "reading group," and the basal texts are chosen to meet their reading level needs. The reading period usually finds the teacher working with each group independently in an attempt to help the youngsters arrive at a skill level that is thought to be acceptable. The practice has merit, as far as it goes.

Some of the assumptions that undergird this practice can be questioned, however. The reading groups that are formed are an attempt to meet individual differences. Yet, these individual differences are supposedly being met by one instructional resource, the basal reader. Can one book meet all the individual differences in a reading group? There are usually many and varied reading problems existing in each group. There are usually many different causes when children are having difficulty with the reading skills. Yet, with the basal reader, we expect the book and workbook to meet all their reading needs and cure all their reading ills. Can we honestly expect one resource to do it all? Are the basal readers *really* meeting the individual differences that we know are so important in helping children learn to read? Can Bill's problems of maturity, Jane's low intellectual level, Roger's problem with basic language development, Alice's slower development of the eye muscles, and Steve's emotional problems all be met and successfully worked with in one low reading group using one basic reading text? Can any cluster of children have their individual reading needs met with one instructional resource? Examine your class, or a group of children that you know, and answer that question. The answer seems obvious. Individual needs need individual help. A hospital certainly will not depend upon just aspirin to cure the many maladies found within its walls. Can we expect one basal reader to cure all our reading ills?

In our age of mass media, where the excitement and color of

the entire world is electronically placed in our living rooms, where travel from one continent to another can take place in a matter of hours, and when the information explosion is affecting all of us, even the youngest, how is the content of many of our basal readers keeping pace? Unfortunately, in many cases, it is not. Too much of the content of the basal readers is hopelessly dull. We are often frustrated as teachers when we attempt to get Ronnie's interest really involved in his basal reader when only last night he watched the World Series on the television at home. Maybe we need to examine why we cannot get his interest stimulated. It is difficult to compare the interest level provided by the World Series with a vapid story perhaps called "New Skates for Ginger." The story of visiting a harbor with, say, "Uncle Charlie," to see how the tug-boat works, written in the language of many basal readers, is somewhat bland and forced when we compare it to a real and immediate adventure of what is going on in the world outside the textbook.

One of the major drawbacks of the basal reading program, especially for the child who is forced to read these books, is that many times they are deadly dull. If one is fed a diet of nothing but stories from the basals, it is somewhat easier to understand why some adolescents and adults dislike to read. If these are the only stories they have been exposed to while learning to read, our work as teachers is in danger of being wasted. While it may be true enough that they can read, the real question should be "will they?"

The slavish use of the basal program can stop or at least stunt good, creative teaching. The imaginative, creative teacher who looks for new, different, and better ways to help children learn will be stifled by the exclusive use of the basal reading text.

Along with the reading text, the publisher furnishes a teacher's manual or guide. Often these guides are so specific and so exacting that real teaching stops and something akin to programed teaching, or teaching by robot, takes over. Some of these guides actually indicate dialogue that should take place between students and teacher. Guided reading is so controlled that the teacher need not even read the story being presented to the children—which may be a blessing in disguise. The workbook assignment is indicated, replete with written instructions for the teacher to *read* to students so that the program may go on as directed.

Directions as specific as these insult the professional competence of a teacher. One may assume, after reading these directions, that the teacher knows nothing about the teaching of reading and, indeed, she is incapable of talking with her students. These series of "reading recipes" are designed to create readers. The teacher that follows these reading guides or manuals in a slavish way is probably the poor soul for whom these guides were written. Most teachers, happily, use them only as guideposts when they feel they are necessary.

Many of the users of a basal reading program expect it to reach universality in that it can do all things in a reading program. The facts are it cannot. No matter how well organized and how detailed, no matter how sequential the program has been developed and the skills reinforced, the basal reading program is not a panacea.

The author's introduction to most of these programs is precise and honest. They have offered a program to develop reading skills. They make no statement about a panacea! They usually point out that the program they offer is not a panacea. It is the use of this basal material by teachers that causes the problem. We expect too much from a program that offers a lot—but not everything.

## THE INDIVIDUALIZED READING PROGRAM

In an attempt to cure the ills of the basal reading program, a new approach emerged that denied all that the basal program offered. It denied the effectiveness of the basal as a foundation for reading and discarded ability grouping. It looked at the needs of the individual in the reading process and attempted to meet them on an individual basis. The basal reader was replaced by children's trade books. The instructional resource was a well-stocked children's library. The approach was called "Individualized Reading;" sometimes it was called the "Self-Selection Program."

The Individualized Reading approach attempts to focus attention on each child by allowing him to select his own reading materials and then giving him an opportunity to confer with his teacher for instructional and diagnostic purposes, alone or in a small group. This program, operated according to the tenets of its disciples, would offer the teacher and student maximum flexibility in a reading program. It would permit the teacher to adjust reading instruction to individual abilities, interest, and needs of the students. The youngster would have a reading program designed for his own reading needs. The pre-planned lesson of the basal reader, the universality that the basal reader attempts to achieve, and the rigidity of the basal approach were to be shucked off and replaced by the individual approach.

The devotees of this program assured us that if the Individualized Reading program were used and the basal reader was exchanged for a wealth of good children's trade books, magazines, and the like, reading instruction, and thus learning, would improve. With the individualized approach, we are told, the child will:

1. Progress more rapidly than he has with the basal approach because he will not be hindered by group instruction techniques and because the program will be "tailored" to his individual needs.

2. Attempt to achieve self-improvement more readily and avoid personal frustrations because he will not be compared directly with others in the group.

3. Read more extensively and widely because he will be allowed to choose his reading material from a wide range of choices provided for him.

It seemed reasonable that we might have an improvement over the old basal approach, after all. The program did offer a real concern for the individual and his reading problems and needs. It did give youngsters a chance to read material that was designed to delight them. The skills were to be taught as teachers found the needs for them within the student. The whole reason for teaching reading came into focus. This approach could very well develop readers of books, not just those that know how to read. Children's literature would have a central place in reading instruction and not be relegated to a role where it may be used after all the "important" tasks are completed.

Programs were designed and research studies followed. Devotees of the program became missionaries carrying "the word" to teachers and schools across the land. A new panacea was found. This was "the way," some told us. The wiser of the missionaries told us that this program offered more than the basal program, but promised no panacea. It was something for teachers to think about and try. It was a new approach with some fine educational thinking behind it. It looked very good on paper and worked well under controlled conditions. It certainly was worth thinking about.

One well-known study, reported in *The Harvard Report on Reading in Elementary Schools*,[1] did indeed give us something to think about. The study was a carefully controlled, well-documented report of reading practices in more than a thousand public schools in this country conducted by Harvard University and supported by the Carnegie Foundation of New York.

The study, which may be representative of others, told us that while this program looked fine in its theoretical state, teachers and administrators who were asked to work with it overwhelmingly rejected it after they had used it for the prescribed period of time. Of the 407 persons polled in this study, 350 did not favor this approach at all. Twenty-four of those that worked with the experiment did like it, and twenty-six were not sure but thought it might work with certain modifications.

Why, we might ask, did the group involved with this study so overwhelmingly reject this practice when it seemed to have such fine possibilities? Why would a group of practicing educators turn down so promising a technique?

The Harvard Report gives us some insights into the reasons why. The following points may indicate why so many administrators and teachers avoided the Individualized Reading program in its pure state.

1. Too few teachers in the study possessed the ability or knowledge to work with this technique in an effective way. A sound knowledge of children's books plus a real understanding of teaching reading is a prerequisite in the program.

---

[1] Mary C. Austin, *et al.*, *The First R, The Harvard Report on Reading in Elementary Schools* (New York: The Macmillan Company, 1963), p. 88.

2. There was an inadequate supply of children's trade books available to students and teachers.

3. The teachers felt that the reading skills were presented in a "haphazard" way.

4. Class size was too large to work effectively with this program.

5. If enough trade books and good, trained teachers were available, many thought they could support the program.

6. The approach was good, it was felt, for academically talented students. It was not, however, good for the average or slow student.

7. The program was a good one for "supplementary" reading, but not to replace the basal program.

8. The approach would be good after the reading skills were taught but not before.

The report continues to analyze the design of the study and to point out questions that were not answered. The basic objections to this program, according to the study, were (1) teachers were not trained to work with this approach and (2) there was an inadequate supply of trade books to carry on the program to completion.

The study cited is, of course, one of many. Some support its findings, others do not. The Individualized Reading program has been modified, changed, programed, written about, and discussed so much that to define it, as it currently exists, is almost impossible. Hundreds of variations are being played on that one theme. The fact remains, however, that this program appears not to be popular with the classroom teacher, and no matter what the research, what the university or the administration say about its value, the classroom teacher has the final word on its use with children.

The program is failing to attract classroom teachers in great numbers because of the reasons outlined in the study cited: (1) teachers do not know how to effectively use it as a method of teaching reading and (2) not enough trade books are found in the average classroom to support the program. Its real value, then, is less than one many think. Theoretical value is, in this case, a far cry from the value of practical application.

Publishers have brought modified Individualized Reading programs to the educational market place as teacher's manuals which discuss book plot and skill development along with a selection of trade books designed for different grade levels. These tools have been a help in giving the teacher a pillar to lean on when attempting to use this program. Other modified programs that can aid the teacher in working even more effectively with this teaching method will undoubtedly develop.

It is clear, however, that the Individualized Reading program has its weaknesses, too. Most of them are in the strategy of operating the program. The strengths are many. It is clear, however, that this approach, the reverse of the basal program, is not a panacea, either. Few thinking educators ever expected it to be.

## THE BEST OF BOTH

The dilemma of helping children master the skills of reading so that they *can* read and developing within these children attitudes toward reading so that they *will* read once we have taught them how, is a real one. No single approach seems to be the panacea, the method, or the answer. Each approach has its strengths and its weaknesses. The reason for helping children learn to read remains, however. We want our students to have more than just the skills of reading; we want them to be readers. We want them to know the value of books as a source of both pleasure and information. We know that the ultimate goal of any reading program is to produce people who will read.

It seems reasonable, then, that as professionals in the field of education, we can tap all the sources available to us. We can take the best from all approaches and use it to fit the needs of our pupils as we see them. Yes, skills must be taught! There are few who would disagree with that. This skill development is a very difficult and complex task. Few teachers, left to their own devices, have the time or the professional background to properly develop these skills. It is obvious, then, that these teachers need professional help from experts in the area of developmental reading. The

*23*

help is available and should be used. The basal reading program's major strength is skill development. It should, then, be used for that purpose.

The reading program should, however, not stop at skill development. It should help children learn that the skills have application beyond the text and the workbook. It should introduce children to literature and give them time to read these books in a classroom setting. It should encourage reading—real reading—beyond the level of skill acquisition. This is certainly one of the strengths of the Individualized Reading approach or the Self-Selection method. That certain skills can be developed by having youngsters read the trade books is an extra benefit; that is undoubtedly on the plus side of the reading ledger. That the skills we are teaching have an opportunity to be exercised and strengthened when children read trade books seems too obvious to mention.

The real value of this method from the writer's point of view is, however, to introduce children's literature as a regular part of the reading program. Its value is that it permits children to really read as we are teaching them to read. It gives children an organized, sanctioned opportunity to interact with good children's books in the classroom. Here is where the real reader is developed. He is given an opportunity to find that the skills of reading have application in an area that will provide adventure, escape, answers, delight, and pleasure. He is able to discover that reading is a wonderful, worthwhile skill that he can use profitably.

How does one go about combining these many approaches into a program that will help children learn the skills of reading as well as help them develop good attitudes toward reading? The possibilities are endless! The creative, imaginative teacher can design dozens of programs combining the best of the various approaches. Very likely one valid approach, among others, would be to organize the reading schedule so that reading of trade books would become a regular, expected part of the reading program. The reading groups or clusters could meet several days a week for the needed development of skills. During this time the basal reader or other device could be used to help children learn those skills and controls necessary for reading. The other days may be set aside for recreational reading where the teacher may bring the reading groups together to share and discuss the trade books they are reading. At this time the teacher can discuss, share ideas, and suggest other books that the youngsters might want to read. At all costs, however, the recreational reading time is considered a regular part of the reading program and is not thought of as a "free time" activity to be done when all the other "valuable" work has been done. At all times, also, a good, varied, and interesting collection of children's trade books is available to the children.

Any program, of course, must be designed for the learning needs of the children concerned. To offer a "recipe" or a "method" here would defeat the purpose of this text. Each classroom is a unique group. What is valid for one classroom may not be for the next. To offer a program that can be used by all teachers and all groups of children is a task yet to be successfully completed. It is a task that this writer will not approach. The purpose of these remarks is to offer a rationale. The professional teacher may then design a program that will best meet her student's needs, based upon that rationale. Curricular development should, in part, be the job of the classroom teacher. It is she, after all, who most affects the learning of her students. Imposed curricular design is seldom as good as that which the classroom teacher designs using a rationale that is educationally sound.

The conscientious reading teacher has a great deal of help available when she begins to design her reading program so that it includes children's literature. The profession of education has a wealth of information concerning the teaching of reading. The sources at the end of this chapter, and in the bibliography of this book, serve only as the first step, as a beginning, in the search for a reading-literature program that is tailor-made for a particular classroom of children. The search can be a delightful, professionally enriching experience that can only leave the searcher more professionally adequate.

## LITERATURE AND THE REMEDIAL READER

What role does children's literature play in helping the retarded reader learn to read? How does literature for children enhance the role of the teacher of the youngster who for many reasons does not grasp the skills of reading? Does children's literature have a place in reading remedialogy?

One must first ask what causes the remedial reader. Why is the youngster having problems in learning to read? This question is usually answered by two generalizations. If the youngster has sufficient mental capacities to read and the physical qualifications to let him read, but is having problems learning, it is likely that (1) his background of experiences and his cultural setting are such that he is at a disadvantage with language skills, one of which is reading, and (2) his own unique learning pattern has not been utilized; he has been taught in one manner but he learns in another.

These are gross generalizations. Each of the two suggested areas above have ramifications that are vast and complex. The probability, however, is that most remedial problems can be grouped under those two general headings.

If the remedial problem is one that the youngster is coming to school with an insufficient experiential background which will not permit him to cope with reading and language instruction, children's literature does indeed have a place in helping him learn to read. As we noted earlier, studies have shown a clear relationship between a rich literature program and language (reading) growth. Reading aloud to children, providing opportunities to interact with children's books on a one-to-one or a one-to-group level is most valuable in helping children develop a language background that will enhance their reading instruction.

Enrichment reading is a practice that is usually advocated for superior readers in a school with culturally disadvantaged students. It is advocated, too, for those with lesser reading abilities.[2] A wealth of trade books, in a remedial situation caused by cultural deprivation, is a fine investment. The trade book is an instructional resource that we cannot afford to overlook.

For the remedial reader who has developed problems because the approach we are using seems not to "take" in his case, a literature-based program may have value. If the youngster is not learning by the traditional methods, or by interacting with basal

---

[2] Dorothy A. Cohn, "The Effect of Literature on Vocabulary and Reading Achievement," *Elementary English*, XIV (February, 1968), p. 213.

material, it may be wise to consider another approach. If the basal system has not proved satisfactory for several years, the possibility exists that it will not prove satisfactory in the next few years, either. Should we keep applying a method that does not seem to work? Should we not attempt a new, different, and perhaps better method to help him learn to read?

Children's literature, as a way of teaching reading, may well be one way of helping him. Perhaps by finding his interests, hobbies, aspirations, and desires, we can capitalize on them and provide trade books that can offer him such valuable information or pleasure that his attempts at reading may take on new energy and help him overcome his problems.

The writer remembers one such case when he taught the fourth grade in a suburb of San Francisco, California. Tim was a retarded reader. His dislike for reading was long established by his inability to cope with the requirements of the basal. He staunchly refused to "try," as his cumulative record showed, and his parents agreed. The reading specialist who worked with remedial readers was likewise in a quandary of how to help him learn to read. This became very apparent to me, as his teacher, when we met to read. Early failure had ground its mark into his attitude. The basal reader, geared for several grade levels below his interest level, had little attraction for him. He simply blocked at reading. The reason for it baffled all of us.

Tim, however, had an interest—really more of a passion—for model airplane building. He had his bedroom festooned with all manner of model airplanes that he and his father, an airplane buff himself, had constructed. Photographs and drawings of airplanes decorated the walls. He would often share his knowledge on the subject with his classmates during the share-and-tell time, and he would instruct on model building whenever he had the chance. His vocabulary far exceeded mine in this area, as did his basic knowledge. His conversation about his hobby bordered on the esoteric.

In our school's collection of trade books, there were several low-vocabulary, high-interest, profusely illustrated books on airplanes. I checked them out and took them to class with me.

Tim's attitude toward the collection of trade books on airplanes remained aloof. He scarcely examined them. They were, after all, books. He had little time for them.

A classroom discussion was engineered toward airplanes and the nearby airport. The students shared information about trips they had taken, the planes they had seen, and the many values of air transportation. Tim's comments were, as always, most valuable. The students listened to him as they would to an expert.

During the discussion, I brought the collection of books about airplanes to the attention of the class. We examined some of them, as a group, and discussed them. They were well-done, well-illustrated, and caused considerable comment. After some discussion, however, Tim announced that they did not tell the entire story. Newer planes were being designed and built that made these planes somewhat obsolete. The earlier planes that developed into the ones shown in the books were ignored. The whole story was not told, he said.

We listened, as always, to Tim's comments on the airplane. He knew the subject and was confident in his ability to share information.

I suggested that Tim take "a look" at these books and come up with some ideas about how they could be improved. What was missing? What should we know about the airplanes that was not in the books? I recommended that he take them home and talk about them with his father and bring some recommendations back to share with the class. This he agreed to do.

The next day Tim arrived with pictures, models, drawings, and magazines. He presented an informal talk that lasted about forty minutes. We were all fascinated. He did, indeed, tell us where the books were weak and what was missing. While he talked, I took notes. When he finished, a summary was placed on the chalkboard and we read it. It amounted to a primary reading technique called an "experience chart." As the children read it, Tim became most interested and on occasion corrected the statements in the summary. He was trying to read!

The remedial teacher, and we were lucky to have one, took the cue, and airplanes were the order of the day for Tim's reading sessions. The trade books, magazines, and model kits became his instructional material. Reading instruction became a time of value for Tim. The books offered to him were a reason for reading. He began to learn to read.

Tim, incidentally, was graduated from a large state university with a degree in engineering. He is employed by the aircraft industry. Evidently the instruction in remedial reading in the fourth grade was sufficient to help him unlock words and put their meaning to use.

## CONTROLLED VOCABULARY

The teacher who is concerned about the remedial reader and wants to help him overcome some of the problems that cause his retardation in the reading area may want to examine some of the controlled vocabulary books that go under the general heading of "trade book." While some may disagree with the term "trade book" applied to the controlled vocabulary books (and for good reason), they are nevertheless available as an instructional resource somewhere on the spectrum between literature and the basal devices.

These little books are written in a graded vocabulary appropriate to the youngster's functional reading level. They are designed as reading aids, *not* for their literary value. Thus, in a true sense, they are not children's trade books. Some teachers, however, wanting to get away from the basal and fearing the trade book approach at that particular time, with a particular child, will use the controlled vocabulary books as a middle stage between the two. Many teachers have found success with them. Many use them as a way of getting children ready for the trade material. It is an area to consider.

Some of the controlled vocabulary books give the retarded reader a real sense of accomplishment in that he can read "the whole book" and then go on to another. Many have high interest levels that complement the low vocabulary and are a welcome break from the "Dick and Jane syndrome" that haunts remedial readers in so many instances. As an attitude builder, as well as a skill builder, many of these books do have merit. They should not, however, be confused with children's trade books. Their purpose is entirely different.

The retarded, or remedial, reader is a problem that has plagued reading teachers since the invention of print. To hope to find the answer to all reading needs within one method or approach, to this writer at least, seems somewhat naive. A reader's learning pattern, his maturity, his background, his attitude, his intelligence, and his physical well-being are all part of the large mosaic that makes him a remedial reader. The one method or one approach that will meet all reading needs is indeed eagerly awaited. It is suggested, however, that it will be a very long wait before that single answer is found. A long wait, indeed.

One approach to help the remedial reader, however, is the trade book. It may capture his interest, may spur him on to greater effort, and may be a good way of helping him cope with the problem of unlocking words. It is an approach that is worth considering. It is an approach that will appeal to the creative teacher.

## Summary

IT SEEMS APPARENT, when we examine the reason for the teaching of reading, that children's trade books should be an integral part of every good reading program. We are teaching reading, one hopes, to open up the wonderful world of books to children. We hope that through our teaching, our students will fully realize the wonder of the printed page. We work so that our students have skills which will help them utilize the universe that is contained in print. It is our desire to develop readers, not just people who know how to read. The wonderful world of children's literature is a vital, necessary instructional resource that can help us achieve our goals.

As teachers of reading, how can we go about making literature a regular part of our reading instruction? How can we arrange our busy schedule to provide an opportunity for students to use the reading skills we have given them? How can we go about creating an atmosphere that will let students read in the class-room? What can we do in the classroom to develop readers of books?

First, and above all, is our attitude about the role of reading—real reading—in the classroom. If we help students understand that the purpose of developmental reading and the acquisition of reading skills is to give them the key to the world of literature and all its wonders, we have moved forward, indeed. The library, or the library corner, should not be a place for free activity alone, or an extracurricular activity. Instead, it should be an interesting place to which children can go often, expecting to find an exciting, changing collection of good books. It should be a place of adventure and delight where children are encouraged to hunt, browse, and explore. It should be a place where he can choose books that will give him answers or provide delight. Weekly book talks can attest to our attitude about books. By our attention to a good trade book in the book talk, we indicate the worthwhileness of children's literature. Children are affected by our attitudes toward things. That is part of the way they learn. The way we view the role of children's literature as part of their lives does a great deal in teaching them the value of reading that literature.

Special and adequate time for reading is vital in helping children become readers of books. Recreational reading is not to be considered a haphazard, spotty activity, or suitable only for out-of-school reading. We can assign regular times during the school week to trade book reading. Often two regular reading periods can be given to recreational reading, leaving the other three days of that period to basal devices and skill building. These periods of recreational reading can be part of the class routine—to be expected with the regularity of arithmetic, spelling, and social studies.

Reading aloud by the teacher to the students is a delightful way to open the world of literature to children. Oral reading is important not just to primary grade students but to upper grade boys and girls as well. To interact with the hero of *Call It Courage*, *Island of the Blue Dolphin*, *The Biggest Bear*, *Charlotte's Web*, or *Tom Sawyer*, to name just a few, by listening to the teacher read is a surefire way to create excitement about books and to entice children into reading them. Reading a chapter a day, after lunch, for instance, can certainly whet the reading appetite by giving children new insights into good literature.

We, as teachers, have the important and responsible privilege of giving children the gift of reading. A large part of this gift must be accepted in the form of skills and controls that are taught in a developmental, sequential manner. However, as teachers, we are responsible also to see that this gift of reading is used. It takes time, perhaps, to evaluate our reading programs and find just what opportunities we are opening up so that our students can become readers of books, not people who just know how to read.

# EXERCISES
## FOR THE TEACHER

1.  Visit a classroom in an elementary school. Notice the collection of children's literature available to the youngsters. Find out, if possible, if they are used as a regular part of the reading program.

2.  Discuss with a professional teacher, or a classmate, the real purpose for helping children learn to read.

3.  Ask a youngster to tell you about his after-school activities. Relate these activities to the need for class time for recreational reading.

4.  Find a book about individualized reading practices. Read the rationale for this practice and note teaching strategies. Prepare a lesson plan for an individualized reading lesson.

5.  Examine a basal reading program. What is the interest level of its contents compared to the contents of children's literature of comparable reading difficulty?

6.  Discuss the probability of finding a panacea for all reading ills.

7.  Discuss how a remedial reader can be helped to learn to read more successfully by using trade books as regular reading tools.

8.  Interview, if possible, a reading specialist at a university or in a school system. Ask him to discuss the roles the trade book can play in helping children learn to read.

9.  Interview a child and ask him when he has time for recreational reading. Ask him how the school can provide more time for his reading.

10. Recall your childhood experiences with literature in the classroom. How would you modify this for practice in today's classroom?

11. Make a list of twenty examples of children's literature "too good to miss" for a specific grade level reading experience. Compare your list with others.

# SUGGESTED READINGS

Ashton-Warner, Sylvia. *The Spinster*. New York: Simon and Schuster, 1959.

Austin, Mary C., and Morrison, Coleman. *The First R, The Harvard Report on Reading in the Elementary Schools*. New York: The Macmillan Company, 1963.

Chambers, Dewey W. ". . . Let Them Read," *The Reading Teacher* (December, 1966), pp. 254–57.

Cohen, Dorothy A. "The Effect of Literature on Vocabulary and Reading Achievement," *Elementary English*, XIV, No. 2 (February, 1968), pp. 209–13.

Dresden, Dorothy. "Use and Misuse of Workbooks and Teachers Guides in Kindergarten Through Grade Three," *Materials for Reading* (Proceedings of the Annual Conference on Reading, December 19, 1957), pp. 75–78.

Ellinger, Beatrice D. "Literature for Head Start Classes," *Elementary English*, XLIII, No. 5 (May, 1966), pp. 453–59.

Miel, Alice, ed. *Individualizing Reading Practice*. New York: Teachers College, Columbia University, 1958.

National Society for the Study of Education. *The Sixty-first Yearbook*. Part I: Individualized Instruction. Chicago: University of Chicago Press, 1962.

Nila, Sister Mary. "Foundations for a Successful Reading Program," *Education* (May, 1953), p. 73.

Robinson, Helen F., and Mukerji, Rose. "Language and Concept Development with Disadvantaged Children," *Educational Leadership* (November, 1965), p. 23.

Smith, Henry P., and Dechant, Emerald V. *Psychology in Teaching Reading*. Englewood Cliffs, N. J.: Prentice-Hall, 1961.

Spiegler, Charles G. "Johnny Will Read What He Wants to Read," *Developing Permanent Interests in Reading*. Supplementary

Educational Monographs, No. 84. Compiled and edited by Helen M. Robinson. Chicago: University of Chicago Press, 1956.

VEACH, JEANETTE. *Individualizing your Reading Program.* New York: G. P. Putnam's Sons, 1959.

WITTY, PAUL A. "Interest, Effort, and Success: Basis for Effective Reading," *Education* (April, 1959), p. 480.

*Chapter II*

# CHILDREN'S LITERATURE
# AND THE SOCIAL STUDIES

*The social studies unit*
was an exciting one. It was concerned with the westward trek of
the pioneers in the 1840s and the 1850s. It offered possibilities of
covered wagons, Indian battles, stalwart scouts, trail blazing, mountain men, vast prairies, and giant mountains. The bulletin boards
were designed to whet the appetite of the youngsters for this exciting fare of Americana. They featured colorful pictures of
pioneers, various geographical environments they encountered,
modes of travel, maps showing routes to their destinations, pictures
of frontier towns and villages, and thought-provoking questions
that could lead to a better understanding of man's adjustment to
his physical and social environment at the time of the westward
movement. The setting was ideal. The subject was exciting. The
classroom environment was carefully planned and beautifully executed. The teacher was prepared and unit plans were well-defined.
The children were eager to be off on an exciting adventure of
learning.

As a way to launch into a fruitful social studies unit, it looked
very close to perfect. Here, I thought, was a highly creative teach-

er, quite able to help children learn. What a pleasure it would be to visit this classroom from time to time to watch these children develop concepts and generalizations, to learn about themselves and others through the vehicle of an exciting social studies unit. What a delight it would be to watch this teacher at work, helping these youngsters learn. It would certainly be a valuable learning experience for me, as a professor of education. Few lectures or scholarly books offer the opportunity to understand the art of teaching better than watching a true teaching artist. I was most anxious to return to this classroom.

Several weeks slipped by before I had the opportunity to return. I blocked out an entire afternoon, however, and eagerly drove to the school in anticipation of learning from a master teacher working with her students.

The classroom still looked like the exciting place I had remembered. The physical environment was most colorful and stimulating. The topic of the unit still offered boundless possibilities for the adventure of learning. Yet, somehow, the environment had changed. The almost electric excitement that was present several weeks ago now seemed somewhat less. The meeting of the group for the social studies period did not seem charged with the excitement I had expected. The children were cooperative but the feeling of the group seemed almost like that of a task-oriented group. They seemed willing to go ahead but mainly were eager to "get the job over with." Something was missing. I soon discovered what it was.

The job of this particular day was to gather information about life on the wagon train heading west. The job of information-gathering had gone on the day before and was to continue for several days. The central purpose of the unit was, in fact, to understand about the people and their problems during this migration. This particular section of the unit was concerned with life on the trail.

The youngsters reviewed the learning that had been acquired the day before and were instructed to notice what further insights could be gleaned from the day's lesson. Then they were instructed to begin.

The textbooks were brought out from the various desks,

opened to the appropriate place, and the reading began. The reading was done first by one student and then by another. Even though this method of information-gathering is somewhat less than exciting, it is often used and is valuable as far as it can go. After all, I reasoned, all classroom activities do not have to resemble the Moscow Circus. There are times when information must be gathered before exciting projects and discussions can take place.

The text the group was using was from a respectable publisher. It was well-designed and lavishly illustrated. The style was factual, matter-of-fact, no-nonsense informational writing. It outlined some important events of the westward movement. The text contained more units than the one on the westward movement so that the content about the migration had to be condensed in order to give "equal time" to other units within the book. This is the practice of many social studies texts. They are expensive and a school district often will expect more from its investment than just one unit. This practice does make sense when viewed in terms of the scarce educational dollars and cents available. They are, after all, designed to act as a springboard from which a unit in social studies is launched. They do not pretend to be the entire unit. They are just one instructional resource available to the teacher. Most teacher's editions make this quite clear.

The students took turns reading about the wagon train and its westward trek. The children seemed to be waiting for a spark of adventure or a vignette that would add people, real problems, identification. I certainly was. But the wagon wheels laboriously rolled along.

Finally, the reading reached a sentence that ended, ". . . and they crossed the river." Somehow my mind stopped at that point. ". . . and they crossed the river!" Is that all they are going to say about this? What about the preparation, the problem solving, the danger, the creative use of available material, the "American know-how," the sweat and the fear, the execution of the task, the elation after the completion of the task? What about the people? How did they *feel?* What was *their* reaction? This westward movement was more than just a historical event. People were involved. If we are going to help children understand about man and his physical and social environment, *man* should be a part of the study, not just what he did. This was what was missing. There was no opportunity for emotion here. It was all intellectual fact. The entire issue of emotion as a part of the learning process was missing. There was no chance to identify with these people who developed our land. They, as people, were not involved in the textbook. That text was concerned only with what they did: ". . . and they crossed the river." Indeed! . . . and Hannibal crossed the Alps; . . . and Columbus discovered America; . . . the Pilgrims landed at Plymouth; . . . and Neil Armstrong walked on the moon! This wasn't social studies. This was a "watered down history course." This was a one-dimensional look at some events that led to the opening of our western United States. This was nothing but fact, the lowest level of learning. This was material tailor-made for forgetting. This was social studies learning based upon the textbook alone.

## DEPTH OF UNDERSTANDING

Social studies usually refers to that phase of the curriculum in the elementary school which has a primary responsibility for helping children develop understandings, skills, and attitudes needed for intelligent living in a democratic society. This would include studies in citizenship, civic responsibility, and human relations.[1] "It is the study of man and his interaction with his social and physical environments in the past, present, and emerging future."[2] Social studies is more than just a collection of historical and geographic facts. It should be more than a "watered down" history course.

The content of a social studies unit, however, is the vehicle by which a youngster is able to achieve the desired learning. To be sure, without content, or subject matter, a social studies unit would

---

[1] William B. Ragan, and John D. McAuley, *Social Studies for Today's Children* (New York: Appleton-Century-Crofts, 1964), p. 5.

[2] John U. Michaelis, *Social Studies for Children in a Democracy* (Englewood Cliffs, N. J.: Prentice-Hall, Inc., 1963), p. 8.

be of little value to the curriculum. Of concern to us, then, is how this content is developed and presented to youngsters who are involved in the social studies program.

One of the major concerns about content is that often children do not develop sufficient depth to really understand its importance or its relevance to them. Content in social studies often operates at the factual level not at a level on which a youngster can internalize and can conceptualize the broader ramifications and implications. Facts, of and by themselves, do not lead to understanding. Facts are only tools to be used in learning. By themselves, many facts are meaningless.

It is too often true that social studies is taught only in a framework of facts. The textbook that accompanies social studies is too often a mass of facts with little interpretation of them and few chances for concept development. The authors of these books are usually persons of high scholarship, great knowledge, and good judgment in the area of the social sciences. They carefully select the information to be presented and offer it in an economical, factual style. Therefore, much of this basic material tends to be skeletal, poor in style, lacking any human element and void of much learning beyond the factual level. These books seldom offer any opportunity for identification, emotional reaction, human motivation, human behavior, or knowledge that social growth and social movement are concerned with people—real people—and their attempts to better interact with their environments.

Each of the disciplines of the social studies program is based upon concepts that can be extracted from that discipline and examined. The textbook cannot be expected to act as the only tool in this concept development. By their very nature and format these books tend to verbalize concepts rather than present materials that would aid in the construction of these concepts. Indeed, often the concept is treated as a secondary or incidental condition, tucked neatly away amid the facts. Reinforcement of any concept is ofttimes totally missing.

The social studies textbook simply does not begin to satisfy the curious child. It cannot possibly answer his questions or give insight into the heart of any social phenomenon. It is not geared to help him solve his problems of relationships and values. It is not designed to give him the depth he needs. The youngster wants specific and accurate information, true, but he is more concerned with what is beyond factual information. He wants more than a statement that says, ". . . and they crossed the river." He wants to know how they crossed the river. He wants to know about the people and why they came to that river in the first place. He wants to know about what they left. He wants to know about where they are going and why. He wants to know much more than he is given in a single text. He wants to go beyond the factual level.

This concept building, this depth of understanding that is so necessary in valuable social studies learning, can be heightened and enhanced by the use of good children's literature as part of the social studies program. Good and thoughtful use of children's trade books can undergird and add strength to the social studies program by offering opportunities to deepen the concepts we hope to teach. They can help us take children beyond the facts. They can provide real understanding about why the facts exist and what they mean in terms of the social movements we hope to bring to the awareness of children.

Children's literature and social studies reinforce each other. The trade book is a good instrument for transmitting the mores of a culture and the beliefs of a people. The children's trade book offers a multitude of ways to know and learn about oneself and others. Through children's literature, the child can experience the common feelings of the family of man. Books can help children get to know people and places in their world. They can transport them to other times and other social settings. These books can help children see how man adjusts to his environment and understands the influences that shape it.

As John U. Michaelis states:

> Literary selections are used in the social studies to heighten interest, deepen understanding, create moods and atmosphere, portray the diversity of ways of living and thinking among people in various cultures, stimulate imagination, give colorful backgrounds, promote more complete identification with others (build appreciations for the contributions of others),

provoke creativity, and give vivid impressions of ways of living being studied in various units.[3]

Children's literature, both the realistic fiction and informational variety, can add needed flesh to the skeleton of information supplied by a basic social studies text, or a group of texts. These trade books reinforce and corroborate specific data such as routes of travel, climatic conditions, population distribution, geographic manifestations, and other environmental phenomena. Many good children's books are written so that children can put themselves into the story. As a result, the children can react so strongly that facts and situations can be recalled when they are needed.

By and large, we can expect children's trade books in the social studies program to provide more depth and meaning than can be found in the basic factual material—the texts and general reference books. These trade books really offer another dimension to the social studies program. They offer reality. The trade book provides a spark of life. The people in them seem real. The problems they face have real-life relevance. The social context, or the times, take on meaning.

". . . and they crossed the river" indeed! As I watched that class, I knew it was time to discuss the problems of the trail as seen by the likes of Michael Chester in his *First Wagons to California*, Hildegard Hawthorne in *Wheels Toward the West*, Holling C. Holling in *Tree in the Trail*, or Alfred Powers in *A Long Way to Frisco*, just to name a few of those fine historical fiction books available.

Now would be the time to offer a collection of good children's trade books that tell the adventure side of the western movement. Now would be the time for children's folk literature to portray Americana. This would have been the time to have a book talk, to point out the drama that is in the books about the westward trek. This would have been the time for the teacher to read to the children a good, authentic, well-written adventure story about life on a wagon train moving west. It was time to put

---

[3] John U. Michaelis, *Social Studies for Children in a Democracy: Recent Trends and Developments*, 3rd ed., © 1963, Prentice-Hall, Inc., p. 528.

flesh on the social studies skeleton. It was time to bring depth concept from fact. It was time for children's literature in the social studies program.

## THE EMOTIONAL DIMENSION

Too often teachers are concerned only with the intellectual level of teaching and learning. We are concerned about factual information that children need to successfully move on into the next phase of their education. Quite often concern centers around factual information that can and should lead into the realm of concepts and generalizations. The building of concepts and generalizations in an area such as social studies does demand factual material. It is, and should be, intellectually challenging. While no one can argue with the intellectual level of learning, can we allow learning to stop there? Is it enough, in an area such as social studies, to just "know about" a topic? Should we not consider the possibility of an emotional dimension as well? An emotional dimension that will permit a vicarious empathy, a feeling with the times, the place, the conditions, and the world of the social studies unit? Certainly, the concept depth that is of concern to us could be enhanced greatly if an empathic response could be created in the youngsters we try to influence.

The objectives or outcomes of many social studies units are often in terms of attitude change, social development, or behavior change. Can these objectives be fully developed with intellectual achievement only? Perhaps there needs to be a dimension to accompany this intellectual growth. Perhaps we should consider emotional identification as a necessary part of learning in the social studies.

Certainly the factual skeleton of the textbook cannot supply this dimension. It is hard pressed even to begin to help the development of concepts. To move into the realm of empathic response would certainly tax these basic materials beyond any reasonable limit.

Children's literature is certainly one of the better ways to provide this dimension. Emotional identification becomes highly possible when a good story is provided, be it realistic or historic fiction, with its setting in the time and place of the social studies unit; a biography, offering personal interaction with a great figure of the time and place of the unit; or a nonfiction offering. The unit discussed in the opening of this chapter, the study of the westward movement in the 1840s and 1850s, might be a good case in point.

While the social studies text may offer a framework of fact about the movement of our pioneers across America, the trade book could well provide the emotional dimension that would make the unit a learning experience that could last for years to come. The adventures of the hero in Michael Chester's historical fiction tale, *First Wagons to California,* could well be one source that would provide this adventure in learning. The young hero in this book tells about his overland trip to California in 1844 in a lively and historically accurate narrative. The adventures of the trail are well drawn and understandable. Facts about the trip are evident. Best of all, however, is how this young hero reacted to the adventure. We get to know him. We understand him. We can put on imaginary buckskin and boots and walk beside him as he crosses the prairies, climbs the mountains, and crosses the rivers. We can identify with his concerns, his joys, his hopes, his fears, and his final victory. We can share his food, worry about unfriendly Indians, wonder how to get over the mountains, and learn the rules of the trail with him. We can come to understand that the wagon train was more than a historical fact. It had people—people that offered identification, people like us, and people like those we know.

The young hero offers us a chance to empathize with a social movement of over a century ago. He offers us a chance to develop real depth of understanding about life on a wagon train moving west. He provides us with a dimension of reality that brings social studies content into vivid life that can be understood and appreciated not only at the intellectual level, but at the emotional level as well. The young hero of this book, as heroes of other fine historical fiction books using a similar setting and time, can add the magic of imagination to fact, making the learning experience a vital, alive, creative experience that can affect the learner viscerally. Good children's literature can do much more than tell a delightful story. Good children's literature, used correctly in a setting such as social studies, can enhance learning and make an ordinary classroom experience soar to great educational heights.

## THE INFORMATIONAL BOOK

While many good social studies teachers find realistic fiction, historical fiction, or biographical material available in children's literature a real boon in helping children enjoy and learn social studies, many use the informational book as an effective teaching device, as well.

The informational children's book is not in the fictional tradition, nor strictly in the biographical genre. It is a specialty of children's literature—geared to give a wealth of information in an interesting, readable way to the youngster who wishes it. It is, however, not a resource book in the true sense as it is written in the trade style and tradition meant to delight the reader. Informational books are available to the youngster on every conceivable topic, on all reading levels, and in varying degrees of depth.

The informational book has been used successfully by teachers of science and social studies for some time. These fine books have helped children develop hobbies or special interests since they first came on the market. Youngsters enjoy them and teachers employ them with great success. As enrichment material, they are without peer.

The informational book seems to be especially designed for the young researcher. Many of these books have fine and accurate illustrations, a good, meaty text, a detailed index, a table of contents, and often a glossary, bibliography, and possibly footnotes. It offers the youngster who does research a fine place to begin. It offers him an opportunity to understand how a researcher goes about gathering the data he seeks. These fine books show him, through the aforementioned tools presented in the book, how to use research techniques. It helps him to know that all books are not meant to be read from "cover to cover" in order to be of value. A good informational book can expand and enhance the youngster's ideas about what books are and how they can be used.

The children's informational trade book is a valuable source for any social studies unit. Many of these fine books allow children to go in depth, far greater than most texts will allow, when searching for information to solve problems in social studies.

*School setting: Lincoln Elementary School, Stockton, California*
PHOTO: APERTURE LIMITED, STOCKTON, CALIFORNIA

hung her stewpot over the fire on a wooden pot-hook (a duplicate of the Indian one) from a lug pole set across the inside of the chimney. This pole was put in green so it wouldn't burn readily, and her husband had to renew it at intervals, as it dried out in the heat. In addition to the indispensable pot, a bake kettle, an iron skillet with three legs and a long handle, a gridiron for broil-

the top, was pounded with a pestle ten feet long and six inches thick. The pestle was so heavy that help was needed to lift it, so he hung it at the end of a limber pole called a sweep. Using the handle that passed through the pestle a couple of feet from its bottom, two people could work together, banging the pestle down and letting it spring up again.

*Sheet-iron corn grater*

*A trencher and a wooden spoon*

ing, a long iron fork, a ladle, and perhaps a strainer would complete the utensils list of the best equipped kitchen in the woods.

*Bake kettle*

### FOOD

Neighborliness may have extended to lending a little corn to new settlers, but there wasn't always enough surplus to permit it. The newcomers watched their own first crop anxiously for the "roast'n' years." Fresh green corn is good even to the well-fed, but these starch-starved folk ate it in a kind of ecstasy. They still ate it when it reached that half-hard state that is neither green corn nor grain; then they crumbled the kernels by rubbing the ears on a homemade grater.

When the corn grew too hard for the grater, the settler broke it up in the hominy block. This was a mortar, given its name because its prime use was for crushing fully hardened kernels that had been hulled by soaking in lye. The settler made his hominy block by burning a round-bottomed cavity into one end of a three-foot log. The log stood on end and the corn, placed in the hole at

*Stewpot, skillet, and gridiron*

25

Edwin Tunis' *Frontier Living* is an excellent example of how the informational trade book can undergird and extend social studies concepts. This book is just one of many that can make social studies a real adventure in learning.

Reprinted by permission of The World Publishing Co. from *Frontier Living* by Edwin Tunis. Copyright 1961 by Edwin Tunis.

The opportunity for cross-checking information, or using several sources to arrive at a conclusion, is a valuable language skill that is often developed or enhanced through the social studies program. Many times, the informational book is the source that expands and rounds out the data that comes from the text, encyclopedia, or other reference material. That youngsters are given an opportunity to seek several authorities to confirm a fact is a large and important step in the direction of developing scholarship. The possibility that the cross-reference checking will provide the youngster with conflicting evidence is an exciting educational possibility. What a fine opportunity for teaching when the sources for gathering data do not agree. What a fine chance to have children examine a book for clues of validity—copyright date, knowledge and background of the author. What a perfect time to help children know that because something is in print, it does not necessarily indicate truth. What a valuable experience it would be for children to compare source material and arrive at a conclusion based upon critical thinking, not just acceptance of the printed word.

The informational book often provides that conflicting evidence. These books, especially those dealing with contemporary society, are usually more up-to-date than the textbook or general reference material available. In a society whose only constant seems to be that of change, conflicting evidence will appear simply as a result of time passage. One needs only to examine the growth of nationalism, for instance, in Africa and Asia to see with what rapidity facts can change. New nations, new ideas, new political directions are evident every year. The text and the encyclopedia are hard pressed to keep pace with our rapidly changing world. It takes several years to produce a text or reference work. Many times they are obsolete at the date of their release. These sources of information will often conflict with material that was produced at a later time, simply because time has passed and the facts have changed. The informational trade book, by its very nature, takes a shorter time to produce and is, therefore, more timely. A check of the date of publication is one way to compare the timeliness of the material. The data contained in the book will offer its own testimony.

The informational book will usually offer more depth and detail than can a text or standard reference material. It can do this because of its limited scope. Not designed to cover the breadth of material that the social studies text is designed to cover, the informational children's book will offer information about, and discuss, one specific area or topic. Likewise, it does not have the broad responsibility of the encyclopedia. The children's informational book is designed to offer real depth in one specific area only.

These books are usually written by, or are under the supervision of, an authority in a special area. Many times these books will be so specific and exacting that the illustrations, for example, will be contemporary with the times or geographic areas discussed.

The informational book is not, and should not be, used as a textbook. It is a source of information to be used by individual children as an aid in problem solving. These books are meant to be selected, used, and paced individually. They are meant to augment and undergird the social studies curriculum but are not necessarily meant to replace the text or other sources of information in that area of the curriculum. Their real value lies in their individuality and the content depth they offer. These books invite children to use them to gather additional needed information for projects or reports, or to answer specific questions. They can feed the interest of the youngsters who want to go beyond the level of fact offered in the basic available materials. As a source of specialized information for children, the trade informational book cannot be equaled. They offer various degrees of depth and reading difficulty so that regardless of the youngster's academic achievement or maturity level, a trade informational book is available to meet some of his intellectual needs.

The social studies unit discussed earlier in this chapter, the westward movement of America's pioneers, cetainly could have profited from the use of a good informational book for additional insight when the children came to that sentence in the text, ". . . and they crossed the river." This could have been the time for a discussion of how this crossing might have taken place. What were the steps in preparing the wagons for this dangerous feat? Did these pioneers look for a certain set of conditions in a river before they crossed it? Did the wagons cross one at a time or in groups? Could the wagons float by themselves or were they modified for the crossing? How long did it usually take to get a wagon train across a river? Did the people (especially the children) remain on the wagons as they crossed?

Such questions often lead to others, and a problem-solving situation is created—a problem that excites the imagination and invites activity to solve it. How good then to know about such fine informational books as Edwin Tunis' *Frontier Living*, among others.

That very fine book, or one of many of like genre, would have done wonders for the development of that social studies unit and certainly would have added depth where it was badly needed. Mr. Tunis in his *Frontier Living* offers a youngster a whole catalog of information about living on the frontier. It discusses everything from flatboats to the Conestoga wagon. Children can learn to churn butter, make quilts, card wool, construct cabins, and even load a musket from interacting with *Frontier Living*. The wealth of information is well-organized and convenient to use. The index is most complete. The illustrations are attractive and accurate and provide additional information beyond what is written. Many times the Tunis materials so engross youngsters that it is difficult to keep the book in circulation. A book like *Frontier Living* is so chock-full of well presented information that once a youngster investigates it, he is reluctant to let it go.

Of course, Tunis' *Frontier Living* is only one of a multitude of superb informational books available to enhance a unit on the westward movement. A browse in a good children's library or a talk with a children's librarian will uncover so many books that a teacher will find it uncomfortable to carry them back to the classroom. The same would be true of any social studies unit. There is a vast number of good informational trade books available on almost any topic. They are there for the gathering.

## SOCIAL STUDIES ACTIVITIES

One of the most successful techniques in the teaching of social studies in the elementary school is employment of activity. This technique provides opportunities for children to cluster in groups so that they may involve themselves in a problem solving learning situation that requires physical activity. Such projects as mural making, diorama construction, dimensional map making, construction of model historical sites, or dramatization have been found to be real aids in helping children learn from the social studies curriculum.

The social studies experts tell us that the activity program provides children with a need for information. If, for example, a group of youngsters is painting a mural about a phase of the westward movement in their social studies class, the group of youngsters is going to need considerable detail about the topic if they are going to portray it pictorially. These children cannot depend upon verbal explanations and abstractions only. They must have the detailed information they seek or their project very likely will not proceed satisfactorily.

Youngsters involved in an activity of this nature will often go to great lengths to get "the facts." That is, of course, one of the purposes of an activity program. The teacher knows that once the youngster's curiosity and imagination have been stirred, he will activate his learning mechanisms and seek answers that will help him solve the problem his project or activity presents. The energy a youngster will exert in a good, well-planned, meaningful classroom activity will surprise and amaze those who will not, or cannot, employ this technique.

The detailed, special information the youngster wishes can be made available to him through many sources. He can use his text material, the standard reference works, motion pictures, slides, recordings, and all the electronic wonders our modern classrooms boast of that have relevance to helping him solve his problem. Among this myriad of aids which will help him find the information he seeks to continue his learning activity should be a good offering of children's literature. There should be informational books, picture books, realistic and historical fiction, and biographical material available to him so that he can use them as his needs direct.

Of particular value to a group of youngsters involved in a mural activity, for instance, would be the illustrations found in many of the finer children's books. Unlike slides, motion pictures, and the like, the illustrations in a children's book are portable and easily obtainable for scrutiny the second, third, or fourth time they are needed. The bonanza of information some illustrations in children's books contain are a source of research material that should not go unnoticed. These illustrations and the accompanying text material provide accurate, precise, and well-presented information by the bushel basket.

The picture book, that special kind of children's book that is a "twice told tale," a tale told once in text and once in illustrations, is another kind of trade book that can enhance learning in the social studies and can be of particular value in an activity program. Children often want to see examples of what they are studying. They want pictures of a general nature and pictures that are specialized in their emphasis. Children learn much from the illustrations in a book. If the book is designed to help children learn through interaction with pictures, so much the better.

Picture books are often misunderstood. Because they are usually oversized and place their emphasis on illustrations, they are thought, by the uninitiated, to be books for only the very young child. This is not true. Many fine picture books, particularly of the historical or realistic fiction variety, have concepts and vocabulary levels that are clearly geared to the upper grades. This is especially true of many informational picture books. A veritable wealth of information that would be of value to many adults is often found in informational picture books produced for children.

These books contain not only fine illustrations but a text that accompanies the pictures to add a still different dimension. Children will look and look again at a good informational picture book. The knowledge they gain from looking at these books can only enhance their education.

In an activity such as the one mentioned earlier, that of painting a mural about the westward trek of the early pioneers, the delightful and information-packed picture book by Holling C. Holling, *Tree in the Trail*, will offer hours of fruitful searching.

*Tree in the Trail* is the story of a tree planted by an Indian child many years ago in our Southwest. The history of our westward expansion revolves around this tree as it grows from a sapling to maturity. Indian life, the coming of the Spanish, the Mexican period, the mountain men, the wagon trains, and all the drama of history touch the tree as time passes. The saga of the westward trek is told beautifully.

Holling presents an accurate, moving, and exciting chronicle of this in the text of *Tree in the Trail*. But what is so outstanding about this book are the illustrations that accompany the text. Holling provides a full page of lavish, colorful illustrations at every turn. He paints an accurate and detailed (if romanticized) episode of this historical drama on every page. From the beginning, when the Indian youth plants the tree, to the end of the book when the tree is cut to provide a yoke for the oxen pulling the wagons to California, the reader can follow this movement in pictures. The youngster, interacting with these pictures, can find enough detail to satisfy many questions and, certainly, enough detail to act as a genesis for new questions.

One technique that Holling uses is of particular interest to teachers of social studies. On the page opposite the color illustration, the page that contains the text of this fine informational picture book, more pictorial information is offered. In the margins of the text page, Holling has included pen and ink drawings, short notes, and postscripts to the reader. These drawings offer a multitude of factual information that is interesting and most precise. So specialized is much of this information that a youngster interacting with it can develop a surprising amount of expertise. The graphic excellence offers more depth and detail in an area than can be offered in written form for children.

In an activity project, such as making a mural, the graphic detail children want is available to them, in this book, in great amounts. The graphic information is there for comparing, to be used as a model, to extend concepts, to be used as an important aid in problem solving.

The author in no way wishes to indicate, however, that the Holling C. Holling material is the only informational picture book available to help children solve the hypothetical problem of making a mural about the westward movement. The book lists are full of such books. The use of the Holling material here is only meant to serve as an example. The search for others will take the reader on a wonderful treasure hunt through children's informational literature. It is a search that is bound to amaze and delight!

## THE BIOGRAPHY

The biography in children's literature is, and has been, a favorite tool of social studies teachers, and for good reason. These books about the great, the near great, and the interesting people in history and contemporary times offer youngsters a chance to interact, on a personal level, with some of the most interesting and important personalities that ever lived. The children's biography should be a vital part of every good social studies program.

To the uninitiated, a biography is not just the story of the life of a famous person. This is true, insofar as it goes. It *is* the story of the life of a person, but it can be more. In good biographical material for children, we can expect more. More is available, if we look for it.

The writer of these biographies for children, or for adults for that matter, must make choices about the material he includes in his book. What aspects of life shall he include, and what aspects shall he exclude? Aside from an interesting story, what did the life of the person he is writing about stand for, in the long run? The life story of a famous person usually exemplifies a point of view, a calling, a movement in history. The story of the life that the biography tells, therefore, can be a vehicle to an idea greater than just a surface life story. As he writes, then, the biographer must choose incidents that will emphasize his case. He uses a "critical incident technique" that will best tell the story as he wishes to tell it. To accept, then, a biography for children as simply the life story of a famous personage is somewhat naive. We need to ask ourselves what the author intended to say as he told the life story. What large truth does the biography offer? How can we use it as a part of our social studies curriculum?

Several examples of this approach to understanding children's biographies can be seen in the following cases:

1. A biography can give the story of a people and a movement in history.
   EXAMPLE: James Daugherty, *Daniel Boone.*
2. A biography can reflect cultural evolution.
   EXAMPLE: Elizabeth Yates, *Amos Fortune, Free Man.*

3. A biography can personalize a cause.
   EXAMPLE: Ernst Schnabel, *Anne Frank, A Portrait in Courage.*

4. A biography can give meaning to faith.
   EXAMPLE: Leo Politi, *St. Francis and the Animals.*

5. A biography can give body to an idea.
   EXAMPLE: Alice Dalgliesh, *The Columbus Story.*

6. A biography can give motion to the facts.
   EXAMPLE: Alden Hatch, *George Patton, General in Spurs.*

7. A biography can mirror the personalities of great persons in history.
   EXAMPLE: Clara I. Judson, *Biography of Andrew Jackson.*

8. A biography can be a story of a way of life.
   EXAMPLE: Henry S. Commanger, *Robert E. Lee.*

The insights that a good children's biography, as seen in this context, can offer to a social studies learning situation are most impressive. Correctly used, the children's biography has an important role in the elementary social studies curriculum.

How can we, as teachers, insure the fact that children will interact with the biographical information available to them in our classrooms? What can we do to bring children and these books together in a social studies situation? How can we help children know what is in the biographies that we offer them? This problem has plagued us for years.

Shall we assign certain books to children and ask for reports, either oral or written, concerning the content and message? Would it be wise to enforce the reading of this material? I think not. One of the best ways to get children to avoid material of this kind is to require it to be read. We also need to remember that this is, after all, literature and not writing of the textbook genre. The attitudes we create about the reading of literature is of prime importance whenever we use literature as part of the content fields. An excellent way to destroy the enjoyment, and thus the value,

RENDEZVOUS (RON'-DAY-VOO)

A French word meaning a place where people have planned to meet — or the meeting itself. Trappers in the Rockies had a famous rendezvous on the Green River in what is now Wyoming. Once each year they rendezvoused to trade among themselves, tell stories, and have a 'rootin' tootin' racin' shootin' wild an' woolly *time !!!*

STAKES.
BOLSTERS.
KING-BOLT
REACH
Blacksmith hammer makes bolt to hold yoke chain.
(ADJUSTS FOR LENGTH)
AXLES
HOUNDS
SPINDLES (WITH PINS)
BOLT HOLE MAKES A 'DROP TONGUE'
DIAGRAM OF FRAME, CALLED RUNNING-GEAR (WHEELS OFF).

RIM
THE WHEEL
The HUB holds SPOKES, which fit into several FELLIES, making the RIM. An iron TIRE holds all parts together.

HOOPS IN BRACKETS
THE WAGON-BOX sits on bolsters, held there by stakes. Wooden strips on outside, chains inside, strengthen walls.

TOOL-BOX
BRAKE LEVER
(pulled by driver with rope or chain)
BRAKE

Bucket with tar for wheel-greasing

THE COVER is an oblong of canvas with drawstrings at ends. When the strings are all tight and sides laced down, it makes a tent protecting the goods inside.

The wagon sketched here is Conestoga type. Types on the TRAIL changed as manufacturers of Pittsburgh, St. Louis, Independence and finally Kansas City re-designed them.

A loaded wagon weighed from 1½ to 3½ TONS and needed about six yoke of oxen, or twelve mules, to haul it across the Plains.

## 20. RENDEZVOUS AT COUNCIL GROVE

Council Grove had the last stand of hardwood on the march westward. Here men made spare parts for their wagons from oak, walnut, maple and hickory. Axes rang, trees crashed, mauls thudded on wedges and logs split open. Hand-saws buzzed, planes and draw-shaves hissed through wood. And the ground was littered with golden curls 'like the floor of a Dutch barbershop,' as Buck said.

Here the men cleaned everything, even themselves. Splashing and laughter rolled along the shady creek. Curious fish swirled through soapy water and swam away in disgust. Crows and thrushes were puzzled when bushes suddenly bloomed with woolens hung to dry.

Small wagon trains came to Council Grove like streams to a river, joining together for better protection against hostile Indians. When a captain was elected to head this larger caravan, Jed Simpson was chosen as usual.

One June morning Jed rolled out of his blankets in the gray dawn to call his first order: 'Catch up! Catch up!' Immediately men raced through the dark to catch and harness their neighing horses, bawling oxen or braying mules. Yoke chains clanked, rings rattled. But soon, from woods and glades, drivers began calling 'All's set!' as their outfits were ready. At the last call, the captain yelled 'Stretch out!' and the wagons rumbled into place in the gray light. Jed standing on a wheel hub, counted forty-one. They were strung out in four rows of ten each, his own in front, like a fleet of sailing ships in a fog, awaiting a breeze.

And Jed X. Simpson supplied the breeze. He carefully smoothed his beard, cupped his hands to his mouth, took a deep breath and bellowed 'FALL-L-L-L IN!' like a bull roaring. Starbright and Bugle lunged against the cottonwood yoke. Men yelled. Whips cracked. And one hundred sixty-four wheels started turning toward Santa Fe.

Social studies research projects can be greatly enhanced by good illustrations found in children's literature. Holling C. Holling's excellent *Tree in the Trail* is a fine example of this. The pictorial information in this book offers hours of thoughtful looking.

An attractive bulletin board featuring dust jackets from
several trade books concerned with the social studies unit
is a good way to whet the reading appetite.
Children's literature and the social studies
reinforce each other well.

of this material is to force it on youngsters and demand its being read.

Rather, it would seem that the creative teacher would try to develop a desire within the children to select this material for reading. Attractive bulletin boards featuring the dust jackets of the biographies is one effective way to create this interest. These colorful and interesting displays can draw attention to what is available to undergird the social studies unit in progress. If the books are available and on display, children may well be drawn to them and reading can result. The "book talk" is another highly effective way to pique the interest of children in books of this nature. Book talks about biographies, with the actual books physically present, will often whet the reading appetites of the youngsters faster than any other technique A teacher who is genuinely excited about the books she is offering, clearly pointing out the features that are of interest and value to students, can be one of the best ways of bringing books and children together.

Most youngsters view their teacher as someone to admire and enjoy and someone from whom they can learn. The attitude of the teacher, as she displays the books in class, is most important to the students. If a teacher is genuinely excited and interested in a type of material this excitement and interest are likely to affect the students. An enthusiastic teacher can, in a figurative sense, infect the class with her own enthusiasm. An exciting book talk, presented by a genuinely enthusiastic teacher who knows what will be of interest and importance to her students, is one of the best ways of bringing youngsters and books together. It is one of the few techniques of which it can be said, "tried and true."

Of course, the oral reading of a biography, or any material that will enhance the social studies unit for that matter, is another excellent and surefire way of bringing children and literature together in a social studies context.

Many teachers find the time after the children return to class from lunch a good time for oral reading. At that time teachers can offer a chapter, a section, or for younger children, an entire short book. Teachers know that it often takes from fifteen to twenty minutes for children to "calm down" after the active games of playtime following lunch. We know it is sometimes difficult to create a climate that is conducive to good teaching following the lunch recess. Teachers who read orally to students immediately after the lunch recess know that a good book is a calming influence that can scarcely be matched. Children often arrive in the classroom ahead of the teacher, place the book open to the material to be read, and sit waiting for the teacher to begin. They do not want to waste time getting ready. They *are* ready. They are ready to listen as the teacher reads.

During this time, the students not only receive the fine literary quality of the book the teacher is reading and content information, if the book is a biography or other material geared to enhance the social studies, but they also see the importance a teacher places on books by taking the time to read to them in class. This demonstration by the teacher of the worthwhileness of children's literature will most likely have its effect. The teacher thinks books are good. She really believes it, and takes time to share them with the children in class. She has other good books about the unit. She has talked about what is in them. They do sound exciting. What better way to get children involved in using trade books, biographies, realistic fiction, historical fiction, informational books, and nonfiction materials in conjunction with the social studies? Once the barrier is broken and youngsters see the validity of literature as a part of their studies, and the teacher allows time for it, social studies will never be the same again. The adventure in good children's literature can indeed be an adventure in learning.


## HUMAN RELATIONS

The aspect of human relations education is an important part of social studies in the elementary school. A curriculum that has, as one of its major goals, the understanding of and appreciation for the various cultural and ethnic groups that make up our United States, is geared to reality. The cultural climate of our country no longer has the leniency it once had for ethnocentrism. It is vital that we help children learn about and appreciate all regions and all groups that comprise our complex society. Some sociologists suggest that the survival of our society may depend upon this kind of learning. The role of human relations cannot be overstressed in the education of the young citizen of the United States.

That the United States is a homogeneous phenomenon, made up of like peoples, like geographic areas, like values and goals, and like styles of living, has been, pretty much, exploded as a myth by scholars of the social sciences. Some even suggest that the "melting pot" concept of American society is likewise fictional. These people would rather call our society a "salad culture."

The term "salad culture" is a graphic phrase in that it describes a society of different elements placed together in close juxtaposition, blending well together, yet remaining intrinsically different. Like a salad in which tomatoes, lettuce, celery and onion are placed together, each ingredient although distinct makes a flavorable course when combined into one dish. So, too, the American people are made up of different groups, yet when combined, make up our nation with one concept. Some social scientists believe that these differences should be valued. It is wrong, they argue, that we seek a blending of our many and diverse peoples; that our strength lies in its diversity.

Regardless of the social science philosophy that appears most valid in the mind of the reader, it is clear that oftentimes groups of Americans are isolated from other groups of Americans. It is also clear that this isolation must be modified and understanding must come in its place. To develop understanding should be the goal of the human relations aspect of our curriculum.

To study the various regions of the United States and to see their likenesses and differences is one good way to begin to develop an understanding of the people who live there. The contrasts between the eastern seaboard and the prairies of the Midwest clearly show how these differing geographic areas affect the lives of the people who live there. Likewise, the contrast of the west coast with our southwest or south points out the same truths. Americans are regional people and regional groups differ from each other, although having much in common. To understand these similarities and differences is an important part of the education to improve human relations. Many children have not had the experience of living in these areas and will gain their knowledge in the classroom. That they acquire an understanding of our geographical diversity and the groups of people that live there is an important goal of social studies education.

The issue of racial diversity is likewise an important variable in understanding the human relations aspect of the United States. We are a "Nation of Nations" made up of people from all areas of the globe. Everyone, including the first American, the American Indian, is an immigrant to this continent, if we are to believe anthropological detective work. We tend to group ourselves, rightly or wrongly, in ethnic or nationalistic groups, often isolating ourselves from other ethnic or nationalistic groups. We are comprised of majority and minority groups of people based upon racial or ethnic guidelines. The efforts to cross these ethnic or racial guidelines, to develop an understanding and an appreciation for each group, is a worthwhile goal of the human relations role in the school's curriculum.

Most social studies materials offer information about the elements of human relations. They discuss regions and point out differences and similarities and they discuss groups of Americans and their respective value despite differences that may exist. These materials clearly point out the value of understanding and appreciating one group for another and emphasize this as a goal in social studies education. The literature of the social scientists clearly makes a plea for the educators of our young to enhance and emphasize this human relations part of our curriculum. By and large, the materials—the text and resource materials available to the teachers—do a fine job.

The job that most of the resource materials and the textbooks do, however, is on an intellectual level. The aspects of human relations, therefore, often take on the role of a clinical, distant, nonhuman study, rather than a deeply-moving humanistic approach. There is little doubt that the intellectual, clinical approach is a necessary one, but can we allow the study of human relations to remain at this lofty plain with elementary school children? Should not this experience in human relations take on a more personal dimension, a dimension that operates not only at the intellectual level but at the emotional level as well, if we hope to change or modify the human relations behavior of our youngsters and gain more positive results? One would hope so.

Certainly good children's literature can fill a large portion of this emotional gap in the human relations study. The fact should not be overlooked that children can be transported, through a good story, into a variety of regional and cultural settings. In a vicarious way, these children can become a part of the lives of the people in the setting under discussion. This, in turn, can produce significant depths of understanding and changes of attitude.

Children's realistic fiction offers numerous chances for children of different groups, both geographical and ethnic, to meet, enjoy, and understand one another. The similarities and differences in their lives, their values, hopes, adventures, and concerns are woven into the better selections of children's realistic fiction. The literary quality of the better books of this genre allows for real identification, identification at the emotional level. It permits an empathic response to people who are different, for one reason or another, from the reader. These books permit children of like groups to understand themselves better, also. They can be a major tool in helping children develop attitudes of human relations that are consistent with the goals of our democracy. These fine books can be an important aid in helping children understand the world in which they live.

Realistic fiction for children, geared to enhance human relations, can be divided into several kinds of offerings. The bibliographies of children's books that are available offer many selections from which to choose. These choices will very likely cluster around such categories as:

1. *International fiction.* Books about children living in cultures other than American.

2. *Intercultural, interracial fiction.* Books about the many racial and cultural groups within American society.

3. *Contemporary American fiction.* Books about modern life in contemporary America.

4. *Regional fiction.* Books about life in specific geographical regions of the United States.

These categories, of course, are not mutually exclusive. Many of the finer realistic fiction books for children will contain more than one category and all are much richer for it. The categories listed above only suggest a variety that teachers may use as they seek to utilize the many fine bibliographies produced for them.

One fine bibliography that no one who seeks to teach human relations through literature should overlook is that by Charlotte M. Keating, *Building Bridges of Understanding.*[4] This fine annotated bibliography offers, at this writing at least, the finest collection of suggested books in intercultural, interracial trade material available. Others are in print, of course, but the Keating bibliography stands alone as a basic source book for teachers who would employ children's books as an aid in helping children gain positive attitudes toward human relations.

The use of children's trade books as an aid in developing positive attitudes about human relations has been extensively examined by some of the most outstanding scholars in professional education. The results of their work have left all of us more knowledgeable in this area. Two of these people have left particularly valuable statements as a result of their work. They are Hilda Taba and Muriel Crosby. (Their studies, with others, will be discussed at length in Section II, *How Books Can Affect Children.*)

Hilda Taba's well-known study, *With Perspective on Human Relations: A Study of Peer Group Dynamics in an Eighth Grade*[5] is a near classic in the field. Taba noted that ethnocentrism and ego-centered persons were very apparent in the eighth grade. One way to help these youngsters extend their social sensitivity and to identify with others and their problems was, she felt, through interaction with literature. Taba, through careful analysis of children's needs, developed a reading program that was designed to extend their social sensitivity. After a year's exposure to this program, Taba concluded that literature and the method that was used did positively affect the youngsters' human relations attitudes and did extend their social sensitivity.

Muriel Crosby edited the most recent *Reading Ladders for*

---

[4] Charlotte M. Keating, *Building Bridges of Understanding* (Tucson, Ariz.: Palo Verde Publishing Company, Inc., 1967).

[5] Hilda Taba, *With Perspective on Human Relations: A Study of Peer Group Dynamics in an Eighth Grade* (Washington, D. C.: American Council on Education, 1955).

*Human Relations*[6] several years ago. It remains one of the most explicit statements available about the use of children's books in developing positive attitudes toward human relations. Crosby's material makes it quite clear that certain children's books contain material that can affect the attitudes of the children who read them. She, like Taba, feels that children's literature is a potent source for the development of these attitudes. The Crosby material, in addition, offers certain titles and suggests what attitudinal learning will result after the youngster has interacted with the books.

The Taba, Crosby, and other materials that discuss human relations education through children's literature suggest that books by themselves are not enough. Discussions, comparisons, and teacher guidance are necessary if the desired results are to occur.

These materials also suggest that not enough research has been done to give us definite, concrete proof about learning human relations through literature. The basic premise, that literature can be a potent force in developing attitudes and values pertinent to human relations, is a valid one.

## Summary

CHILDREN'S BOOKS and social studies reinforce each other. As one way of helping children understand and positively interact with their physical and social environment, children's trade books have an important role. It is a role that cannot be overlooked if we are to offer children rich and meaningful experiences in the elementary school social studies curriculum.

Good children's literature is able to offer depth of meaning when we ask children to formulate concepts and generalizations about a social studies topic. These fine books take children beyond the skeletal facts offered in many standard social studies texts and reference materials. They bring the facts into a meaningful con-

---

[6] Muriel Crosby, ed., *Reading Ladders for Human Relations* (Washington, D. C.: American Council on Education, 1964).

text where people, the times, and the social settings of the unit are brought into vivid life and rendered as a part of an exciting tale. Realistic fiction, historical fiction, informational books, biographies, folk literature, and picture books can often add an emotional dimension to social studies that can take the subject from a purely intellectual level to a level that invites identification and personal involvement.

When the young student employs the trade book in research work and in an activity program, he is given additional, and often badly needed, information to help him complete a successful project. The depth of information supplied to him in these books goes beyond what he can expect from the standard social studies reading materials. The illustrations in the picture books many times offer him what he cannot obtain from the written word. As an aid in research work or in an activity program, the children's trade book is without peer.

The human relations aspect of a social studies program is likewise enhanced by the use of children's literature. The youngster is able to interact with different cultural, ethnic, and geographic groups on a personal level and better understand that phenomenon of diversity within our society. Children's literature offers an emotional dimension to undergird the intellectual understandings that we hope will produce more positive human relations attitudes and behaviors.

For the teacher who is not familiar with the many fine children's trade books geared to aiding and developing the social studies program, help is available. The children's librarian is always a good source of information. She often knows what books are available locally to aid the teacher in developing her program and will many times assist her in obtaining them. Of course, the many fine bibliographies of children's books are a source that teachers cannot afford to overlook. Many are carefully annotated, offer grade or reading level, and are specific about the content. These bibliographies are sources of information about children's books that can greatly reduce the teacher's efforts in finding good books that can enhance the social studies program. Several of the better bibliographies are listed at the end of this chapter and other aids can be found in the bibliography in the back of the book.

It should go without saying, of course, that no matter what aid the teacher uses in locating the trade books to enhance the social studies program, nothing will replace her knowledge of what is in the books she offers to her students. The teacher will be effective, indeed, when she speaks of the books she offers from firsthand experience. Getting that firsthand experience, by reading the books, will be an adventure any teacher will long remember. It is an adventure that, delightfully, has no end.

# EXERCISES
## FOR THE TEACHER

*1.* Examine a social studies text. Find places where the content of the study can be deepened and made more exciting by the wise use of children's literature as part of the social studies program.

2. Discuss why it is important that the social studies offer children an opportunity to really know and understand the "emotional" level of the people and movements involved in the study. Indicate how good children's literature can help fill this void in a social studies program.

*3.* Discuss how fiction, informational books, poetry, folktales, *et al.* can add dimension to a unit of study in the social studies.

*4.* Develop a bibliography of children's trade books that will undergird a specific unit in the social studies. Plan strategies of how these books will be used in that unit of study.

*5.* How does an informational book differ from a textbook? How should the informational book be used in the social studies?

*6.* Prepare a lesson plan for a social studies activity. Note in your plans certain trade books (and illustrations) that will be valuable tools in helping children complete this activity.

7. Defend the teacher's oral reading of children's literature as a valuable practice in social studies. What trade books are good for oral reading in a social studies unit that you are planning?

*8.* How can the use of children's literature enhance the human relations aspect of the social studies program in your school? What problems exist? What trade books are available that will help meet the special needs in your school? How will you present these books to children?

9.  Where in your school, school district, or university can you receive help in developing bibliographies for special social studies problems?

10. If possible, interview the social studies curriculum specialist at a university or in your school district. Ask him to discuss the role of children's literature as an integral part of the elementary school social studies program.

# SUGGESTED READINGS

ASSOCIATION FOR CHILDHOOD EDUCATION INTERNATIONAL. *Bibliography of Books for Children.* Washington, D. C.: Association for Childhood Education International, Biannual.

BAKER, AUGUSTA. *Books About Negro Life for Children.* New York: New York Public Library, 1963.

CARLSON, ROBERT G. *Social Understanding Through Literature.* Washington, D. C.: National Council for the Social Studies, 1965.

CHILD STUDY ASSOCIATION OF AMERICA. *Children's Book Shelf.* New York: Child Study Association of America, 1965.

CROSBY, MURIEL, ed. *Reading Ladders for Human Relations.* Washington, D. C.: American Council on Education, 1964.

DAWSON, MILDRED A. "Literature Enlivens the Social Studies," *Education* (January 1965): 85:294–97.

EAKIN, MARY K. *Subject Index to Books for Primary Grades.* Chicago: American Library Association, 1961.

————. *Subject Index to Books for Intermediate Grades.* 3rd ed. Chicago: American Library Association, 1963.

GUILFOILE, ELIZABETH, ed. *Adventuring with Books: A Book List for Elementary Schools.* Champaign, Ill.: National Council of Teachers of English, 1966.

HARTELL, BARBARA C. "Building Social Studies Concepts Through Trade Books," *Childhood Education* (November 1966): 43:150–52.

HUUS, HELEN. "Children's Books Can Dramatize Social Studies," *National Education Association Journal* (December 1961): 50:44ff.

————. *Children's Books to Enrich the Social Studies.* National Council for the Social Studies, Bulletin No. 32. Washington, D. C.: National Council for the Social Studies, 1966.

JACOBS, LELAND B., ed. *Using Literature with Young Children.* New York: Columbia University Teachers College Press, 1965.

KEATING, CHARLOTTE MATTHEWS. *Building Bridges of Understanding.* Tucson, Ariz.: Palo Verde Publishing Company, Inc., 1967.

MARCKWARDT, ALBERT H., ed. *Literature in Humanities Programs.* Champaign, Ill.: National Council of Teachers of English, 1967.

MICHAELIS, JOHN U. *Social Studies for Children in a Democracy.* Englewood Cliffs, N. J.: Prentice-Hall, Inc., 1963.

RAGAN, WILLIAM B., and MCAULEY, JOHN D. *Social Studies for Today's Children.* New York: Appleton-Century-Crofts, 1964.

ROLLINS, CHARLAMAE. *We Build Together: A Reader's Guide to Negro Life and Literature for Elementary and High School Use.* Champaign, Ill.: National Council of Teachers of English, 1968.

SHORE, RACHEL, and FIDELL, ESTELLE A., eds. *Children's Catalogue.* 11th ed. New York: The H. W. Wilson Company, 1966.

TABA, HILDA. *With Perspective on Human Relations: A Study of Peer Group Dynamics in an Eighth Grade.* Washington, D. C.: American Council on Education, 1955.

*Chapter III*

# CHILDREN'S LITERATURE
# AND THE SCIENCES

*Our era is a scientific one.*
Undoubtedly historians not yet born will regard our age as the
dawning of the scientific period. Man is learning the secrets of matter and the universe so rapidly that he is often unable to relate to
the lives of his fellowmen. The "knowledge explosion" is mainly
concerned with the growth of scientific information. Concepts in
the various fields of science often become obsolete days or weeks
after they have been discovered due to further investigation and
discovery. Some scientists tell us that due to this rapidly expanding
body of scientific knowledge, the only constant one may expect
in modern life is that of change. The scientist, with his technological marvels and approach to finding truth, is the engineer who is
building the new world. It is a world that promises wonders that
stretch the imagination beyond the level of yesterday's fiction.

The work of the scientist, from the beginning of our century
to the present, would boggle the minds of those that lived in the
previous century. Our everyday, accepted, commonplace tools of
living would be suspect and likely attributed to witchcraft and
magic by the people who lived more than a hundred years ago.

The automobile, television, telephone, electric appliances, air travel, space probes, computer services, medical advancements, atomic power, and even mass production would terrify and no doubt would be rejected as supernatural by those who lived in the past century. It would be interesting to imagine how so common a modern phenomenon as a motion picture, for example, would have affected viewers in 1820. The results of such an occasion would likely keep a science fiction writer busyfor sometime.

If scientific prognosis is correct, the change from the present time to the year 2,000 will be even more dramatic than the changes that have taken place in the last one hundred years. The changes that modern scientists promise will indeed reshape our lives. The youngsters we teach in our classrooms today will be the functioning citizens of the culture to come. That they need a scientific education simply to cope with what is to come is self-evident. That these youngsters need a scientific education, so that the contributions necessary to build a better and new world will continue, is imperative.

So important is scientific education today that a very large portion of federal aid to education, as well as a large part of private grant monies, goes into the field of science education. Both industry and government realize the importance of scientific education for our children if our country is to continue as a world leader, or, in fact, just to survive. The "science race" between east and west, on a political and economic level, has emphasized, if not forced, this attention on science education. This area of our curriculum will receive more and more attention as we move further and further into the scientific era.

Dr. Donald McFarland, science educator at the New York State University College at Fredonia, New York, has indicated that pure science, as once taught, has been modified and changed in the science curriculum of today's elementary school. McFarland believes that science should be taught as one of the humanities, rather than as a special, isolated field, unrelated to other areas of the curriculum. Science belongs in the humanities program, he argues, because it is a tool that man uses to understand himself and his world. Science represents one of several ways to see and study the world. The artist sees the world in one way, the social scientist in yet another. The scientist believes that the elementary school should seek a synthesis. It should provide children with opportunities to view their world from several stances. Science is one stance that should provide a view.

## THE ELEMENTARY SCIENCE PROGRAM

What is science? What does a teacher do to help students learn when a science program is offered? What elements should an elementary classroom science experience contain? How would one define "science" for the elementary school student so that it would be both practical and intellectually honest?

Tannenbaum, Stillman, and Piltz offer this definition of science: "The systematized knowledge of nature and the physical world, including zoology, botany, chemistry, physics, geology, etc."[1]

They continue by indicating that the word "science" comes from the Latin word *scientia*, or knowledge. It stands for that which is known. *Scientia* may be contrasted with the Latin antonym, *credentia*, or that which is believed. Science, then, is based upon information which is observable, verifiable, capable of being repeated, and generally agreed upon by a number of independent observers. Science has come to mean the organized body of information—information which has been carefully observed and checked—related to the physical phenomena of the universe. The organized information about the earth and its structure and the generalizations which evolved from this information have become geology. The organized information about plants and the generalizations which grew from it have become botany. In the same way, chemistry, zoology, and physics have come into being. They are the topics around which men have organized bodies of information which they "know."[2]

---

[1] Harold E. Tannenbaum, Nathan Stillman, and Albert Piltz, *Science Education for Elementary School Teachers*, 2nd ed., p. 1. Copyright 1965 by Allyn and Bacon, Inc., Boston. All rights reserved. Reprinted by permission of the publisher.

[2] *Ibid.*, p. 2.

The teachers of science in the elementary school know that the basic laws of learning apply to the teaching and learning of science, as well as to any field. They know that to help students learn, their interest must be aroused, they must have a chance to explore, to manipulate, to "find out" on a primary level and to be involved in the process of science learning whenever it is possible. Teachers know that there need to be many sources of information available to the student who would learn about science. He needs the raw materials of his science experience so that he can see first hand and understand the process of the wonders of the natural world. Should these raw materials be magnets, tadpoles, rocks, levers, or liquids, they need to be present in the classroom so that the student can see, on a firsthand basis, the secrets that science holds. Experimentation and manipulation are basic processes of any science program. Without them, the science program is not complete. The student of science also has the teacher available to him so that he can avail himself of her training and knowledge. The teacher, as a communicator, is a major source of information to the young student of science. He has information available to him in the form of slides, motion pictures, television, and a host of technological aids. He has available to him also the books, both text and trade. The young student of science has a wealth of information from which to draw so that his learning of the sciences will be enhanced. The teacher of science has, as one of her major tasks, the arranging and organizing of those experiences and those sources of information that will best facilitate the student's learning syndrome.

Fortunately, most teachers, through their professional education at the college or university, are given expert and excellent advice on how to arrange and organize good science learning. They are well aware of the necessity for process and discovery, the building of generalizations from specific observable phenomena, and of providing the information children need in learning through their elementary science program. They know the importance of emphasizing the *process* as well as the *product* in a science unit. They are aware of the necessity of science teaching reflecting the nature of science, not just the "history of science" or the accomplishments of science. They are aware that science is one way of viewing the world and it needs to be presented in the light that science is indeed a tool that man uses to understand himself and his world.

## READING AND THE SCIENCE PROGRAM

The complex, involved world of science prohibits any one person from knowing all that is known in the field. The rapid growth of knowledge in each separate area of science forces specialization and fracturing of the areas of science to facilitate the specialization that is developing. For the elementary student of science, this vast amount of information is unfathomable. If he is to learn about the sciences, however, he must be introduced to this vast body of knowledge. Therefore, as desirable as it may seem, we cannot help children learn what they need to learn about science by using the technique of firsthand, primary experiences only. There is simply too much information and not enough time to discover it all in a laboratory situation.

As we noted before, this information is offered in many ways. Films, slides, television, and teacher comments are fine ways to augment and enhance the experimental science program. Far and above all else in the practical format of information-disseminating devices is the written word. The science text, magazines, pamphlets, monographs, and, of course, the science trade books for children are, and should be, an integral part of the science program.

Publishers have provided handsome texts for use in the elementary science program. Well-designed and accurate programs covering the scope of science from kindergarten to eighth grade are available in text series. These books, written, for the most part, by experts in science education, develop concepts and generalizations in such a way that youngsters cannot help but learn from them. They are also a much needed source of support for the teacher who feels less than competent in the science field. They are often beautifully illustrated, contain experiments that can be worked, and provide a valuable bibliography. As an instructional aid, the science texts are valuable for students and teachers alike.

They provide much of the needed information upon which to build an elementary science program.

These texts can, of course, be misused. When they are misused the entire text approach is rejected, by some. The fault lies not in the text, many times, but how it is used. To blame the text for a poor science program is like blaming the water because one cannot swim! The science text is not, and should not be, used as a reader. The uninspired teacher who directs her class to open its science books to page one in September, and plans to finish it in June, working on chapter after chapter as they are found in the text, is of course defeating the whole purpose of the science text. The science text is just one teaching resource. It often serves as a springboard to a project or unit or it serves to provide information in science once the unit is underway. The science text is not meant to be the science program. It is meant to enhance the science program. How the text is used often determines its value. Used correctly, it will be of great value. Used incorrectly, it will hinder learning by imposed rigidity.

The science text, coupled with science magazines for children and the available pamphlets, will serve an elementary science program well. These resources are often the backbone of any science program in the elementary grades.

## THE TRADE BOOK
## IN THE SCIENCE PROGRAM

Because reading for information is an important part of any elementary science program, it would be naive to expect a single text, or group of texts for that matter, even when enhanced by science magazines and pamphlets, to provide all the information a youngster wants and needs once he is underway in a science project. The text is, after all, designed to give a wide breadth of scope covering many fields in a single volume. It is usually written at a level that fits the "average" person at a given grade level. It quite frankly lacks the depth that many children need and want when a science project is underway and fails to provide for individual reading needs because it is aimed for an average student at the grade level, but fails to provide for that large group of children who are above or below the grade level expectations. The text or pamphlet materials, though valuable resources, have extreme limitations. They cannot do all they would like to do, and, certainly, do not provide all the reading information a young scientist needs when he begins to investigate the natural world.

## NEW APPROACHES IN SCIENCE EDUCATION

The new, and often very exciting, approaches in elementary science education, as reflected by the Elementary Science Study, The Minnesota Mathematics and Science Project, and the Science Curriculum Improvement Study, among others, seem to reject the traditional text oriented approach. These new programs would rather have us place the emphasis on the process by which children develop concepts and generalizations about science. The creators of these new science programs know, however, that reading is one process by which children learn. Included, therefore, in most of these approaches (and often one uses a set of "materials" when employing a particular approach) is a wide variety of written materials for children pertinent to the experiences children will have. They are often such materials as laboratory manuals, research reports written at the youngster's level, well illustrated pamphlets explaining one process or the other, and the like. These written materials combined with direct experience are meant to replace the traditional textbook.

The heavy emphasis on experience, and the rejection of the dependency on the textbook in the new science education approaches, make certain demands evident. It points out the need for a rich reading environment that will expand and enhance that which is included in the science materials offered, or suggested, by the approach. A wise selection of children's science trade books, and strategies for their use, will be required by all good teachers who employ any of the exciting, new, innovative programs in science education.

A rich reading environment is needed when
children investigate the scientific world.
One rich source for that reading is the science
trade book. This kind of children's literature
offers the young scientist real scope in his reading.

*School setting: Lincoln Elementary School, Stockton, California*
PHOTO: APERTURE LIMITED, STOCKTON, CALIFORNIA

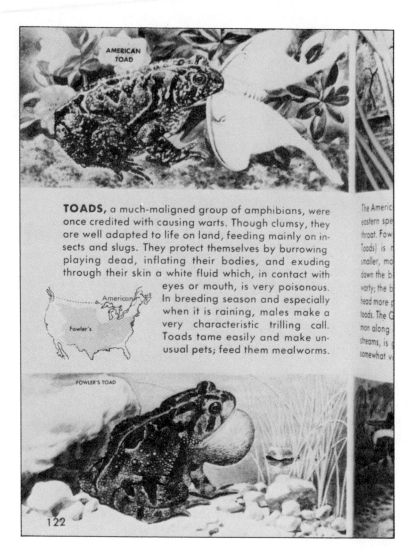

Illustrations in a good science trade book provide excellent opportunities for gathering additional data for a science activity. Those in Herbert Zim's *Reptiles and Amphibians* are good examples.

*Reprinted by permission from* Reptiles and Amphibians, A Golden Nature Guide *by Herbert S. Zim, Ph.D. and Hobart M. Smith, Ph.D., and illustrated by James Gordon Irving. Copyright 1957 by Golden Press, Inc.*

The good and experienced teacher of elementary science knows that a host of science trade books are a necessary and needed part of any science program. These fine books often add the extra dimension that takes an elementary science program from an ordinary learning experience to an exciting, vital learning experience that may start a youngster on an adventure that can last a lifetime. We can expect, from the science trade book, information that goes above and beyond what the text can offer. We can expect the trade informational science book to better meet the reading needs and maturity needs of the student of science. We can expect a more exciting format and a better style of writing from the science trade book than we get from most texts.

The science trade book is one form of literature for children. As literature, one of its major purposes is to delight the reader. That they can delight the reader and provide accurate information is a valid reason for incorporating these books into the science program. We can, however, expect even more from the trade book in the elementary science program.

## EXTENDING AND DEEPENING CONCEPTS BEYOND THE TEXTBOOK

The textbook often acts as a springboard for science activity. It may serve as the stimulus that generates the student into a good learning situation. Many times the text will provide just enough information so that the intellectual appetite is whetted. When the teacher sees the curiosity of a group of youngsters aroused, she is then able to help youngsters go beyond the text so that concepts are extended and deepened. The science trade book is a positive force in this concept extension.

The writer, a supervisor of student teachers, had the opportunity to visit a rural school in central California and spend time with a second grade class. The group was typical of seven and eight year olds. They were active, curious, eager with questions and demanding answers. Their physical needs made the classroom an active, constantly changing environment. The student teacher working with the group often referred to them as "pocket-sized volcanoes." Her description was not far from the truth.

Recess, physical education, and lunch recess gave credibility to the student teacher's description of the group. They literally boiled over with energy and they scattered in all directions on the playground for the large muscle activity they needed. They played on the swings and the bars, they played ball, tag, running and jumping games, and rolled full of giggles on the lawn and in the grass. When the recess period ended, the group reentered their classroom flushed, breathless, and ready for the next group of lessons.

For the first few minutes in the classroom, many of the children picked burrs, "stickers," and dried bits and pieces of plant life from their clothes and sometimes their hair. October in central California is dry and plant life has long since gone to seed. Removing seeds after a recess is standard procedure.

When the large bulk of dried grass and seeds had been removed from clothing and hair and the children returned to their desks, the student teacher commented to one youngster, "Did you get rid of all the hitch-hikers?" The term "hitch-hikers" prompted a shower of laughter and questions.

"Hitch-hikers? What's a hitch-hiker?"
"Hitch-hikers thumb rides on the freeway."
"Brad's not a hitch-hiker—his mom wouldn't let him."

The informal patter continued for a moment or two as the children assembled at their desks. The student teacher, seeming to enjoy the play on words and delighted with the response the comment generated, explained what she meant by the term "hitch-hiker" when she made the remark.

"The 'hitch-hikers' I meant were the seeds that you brushed off your clothing and out of your hair after playtime," she explained. "Seeds are the oldest 'hitch-hikers' in the world. They hitch rides from animals, birds, the wind, and even from people. They hitched a ride from you and got a free ride from the playground into the classroom."

The second graders quickly realized what the term "hitch-hiker" meant in this context. They searched their persons and held up more fugitive "hitch-hikers" to be commented upon and examined.

The resident teacher, more experienced and more able to sense a learning experience in its infancy, commented from her desk that the science text had some interesting things to say about seeds and how they traveled to new spots before they became planted and grew. As a matter of fact, she admitted, she had some plans for a science unit on seeds that would be coming up quite soon.

To the consternation of the student teacher, who had care-fully planned a language lesson for the next period, several young-sters searched their desks for the science texts and produced the section on seeds for their neighbors and themselves to examine. Soon more texts were out and the class was busy examining the pictures and the brief text that accompanied the illustrations. The youngsters were pointing out the seeds they knew.

"Here's a dandelion—it flies."
"Look, here's a 'fox tail.' It traveled on me."
"My dog gives lots of rides. He hates to be brushed."

With an encouraging look from me, the student teacher re-tired from the leadership role and watched the resident teacher take the interest of her students and turn it into a valuable learn-ing situation. She watched as the teacher collected questions from the students about seeds and their ways of travel and formed a series of questions which she summarized on the chalkboard. She then began to question the youngsters about how they could find the answers to these questions. The youngsters, who always will have much to say if we will listen, offered suggestions. They sug-gested, in their own words, some fine techniques on how to solve a science problem. They suggested observation, collection, group-ing according to mode of travel, asking the teacher for informa-tion, watching movies about seeds, watching TV, reading books about seeds, and asking others for information. The teacher noted these ways of getting information about seeds on the chalkboard and continued to question.

"What," she wondered, "would be the best thing to do first?"

The youngsters reasoned that since they had the texts open to the section on seeds sitting on their desks, it might be wise to find out what the book had to say. So, along with the teacher, they bent their heads over the texts to find if some of their questions could be answered by reading.

At this point I was forced to take my leave. On the way to my car, I was able to point out to the student teacher the natural growth of a lesson of this sort and to reassure her that I would be back another time to see the language lesson she had so carefully planned. The kind of teaching ability that was currently in operation would come to her in time, I assured her, but now was the time to watch and learn. I suspected a science unit had been born. I urged her to watch how it grew and to note what techniques and materials the resident teacher would use to make this a real adventure in learning.

When I returned to that second grade the next week, the unit had indeed been born. It was born and was growing into a healthy, active adolescent. Bulletin boards had been placed on the walls— colorful, attractive, and full of information. Children's seed collections were neatly arranged on a central table, each carefully arranged and secured by scotch tape so that their method of travel could be seen. Several planting areas were in evidence, demonstrating what happened when a traveling seed finally became planted and started to grow. The boys and girls were clearly deeply involved in the study. Grass and seeds were no longer carelessly brushed off clothing when they returned to the classroom. Each bit of grass and seed was carefully examined to see if something new had "hitched" a ride. A whole new world had been opened to this group of second graders.

The textbook was still in evidence. Along with the text, however, were numbers of informational children's trade books. The text had become a reference source to be used along with other reference sources, the trade books. A quick look around the room showed a number of these books by the bulletin boards, by the seed collections, and in the library corner. Such titles as Clyde R. Bulla's *A Tree is a Plant*, Millicent Selsam's *Seeds and More Seeds*, as well as her *Play with Seeds*, and Alfred Stefferud's *The Won-*

*ders of Seeds* were among the titles of the informational books in evidence. These books were being used! The children's desks held others that were being hoarded as special prizes by those that had them. They were being used as informational resources because they contained data and material that the children wanted. They were being used as these kinds of books should be used—not necessarily read from cover to cover, but as a way to get needed information.

At the recess break the resident teacher, the student teacher, and I retired to the teachers' lounge for coffee. During that time I quizzed the resident teacher on the development of this science unit. Of particular interest to me was how she used the informational trade book and why. Her answer was clear and simple:

> The text didn't go far enough to give all the answers the children wanted. It served its purpose as a reading springboard, but when the youngsters moved into the unit they wanted more information. I simply telephoned the district librarian and requested the books that are in the room. She knew the ones I wanted. The textbook can only go so far; it must be helped with others—you know—children's science books.

Indeed I did know. The children's trade book, particularly the science informational book, is of inestimable value in helping children learn about the scientific world. The textbook, no matter how fine, does not go far enough—does not go deeply enough into the scientific concepts we would have children learn and understand. It must be augmented by other reading materials. The children's informational trade book is often the tool that provides the depth. Be the book a picture book that offers the concepts in pictures and simple text or be it a more sophisticated presentation for those that are more mature, the children's science trade book can extend and deepen concepts in science beyond what the textbook can offer. To ignore its value is to ignore the principles of modern learning theory.

The student teacher involved with that second grade captured the mood of that learning experience as only a college senior can. "Those kids are so interested in this unit and in those books that they are practically reading the print right off the pages."

## KEEPING ABREAST
## OF NEW DEVELOPMENTS IN SCIENCE

Scientific knowledge is advancing so rapidly that to attempt to keep abreast of it, even in one specialized area, is a full-time job. Unless one is an advanced student of science, involved in sophisticated research in either industry or at the university, he is likely to fall behind in his awareness by simply taking a two-week vacation. To try to keep elementary school students aware of all the new developments in science, as they happen, is an exercise in naivete or frustration. Science educators tell us, however, that one generalization that young science students need is that growth and change in scientific information is a keynote to understanding the scientific era. Advancement and new knowledge will be a constant phenomenon in this age.

The National Science Foundation and other agencies, along with extension and graduate courses at the university and college, attempt to keep the teachers aware of the changes and growth that typify modern science. These fine offerings do much to help the teacher direct her students to this awareness.

One of the operational difficulties for the classroom teacher, however, is to find instructional resources that will aid her in helping students become aware of the changes and growth in certain fields of science. Motion pictures and slides do offer her some help but often are obsolete when they finally become available to students and teachers. Children's scientific periodicals and pamphlets are an excellent source in that they capitalize on current material and do a splendid job of keeping new and vital information flowing into our classrooms for use by those who desire it. The textbook, however, is often hopelessly outdated. As we have noted before, a textbook often takes several years to write and produce. Much information is obsolete by the time the book is released. A set of textbooks is an expensive investment for a school district and many districts simply cannot afford to replace a set with a new revision every year or so. A district will often expect a text, purchased in large numbers, to serve the students for five years or more. Needless to say, by then the changes of obsolescence are more than slight.

An excellent example of this kind of obsolescence would be in developing a science unit based upon rockets and space travel. Too few science texts, except for the newer ones, even mention this important aspect of scientific endeavor. The ones that do include a section on space travel do so from a stance that was valid several years ago and necessarily leave out the newer developments that have taken place since the book was written.

Today's youngsters are keenly interested in, and aware of, new developments in space probes and travel. They accept these scientific marvels with the calmness born of the contemporary. They are quite able to go into considerable depth when it comes to understanding the natural laws and scientific technology that makes space travel possible. Many quite naturally want to go beyond what the text has to say about space probes and will want current material to keep them more abreast of this exciting aspect of the scientific world.

To develop a unit on rockets and space travel by using a text alone would be almost impossible. The current science bulletins, pamphlets, and junior science magazines are a valuable aid, but more substantial reading material is needed. The scientific children's trade book used during a unit on rockets and space is a necessity. They provide more current material than the text often contains, as well as the needed depth of concept and the various levels of sophistication that the maturity levels of any elementary classroom demand. These science informational trade books can serve as a primary source of information for much of a unit on rockets and space.

Publishers have provided hundreds of fine science informational books on rockets and space, for all levels, which cover all aspects of this exciting modern adventure. The book lists are filled with them. A visit to the children's room in a library will deliver armloads of them. They are exciting, well-illustrated, accurate, and well-written. Because a library, school, or school district cannot buy these books in terms of hundreds of copies, they can easily afford the newer ones and thus be able to keep abreast of what is new in the field.

It seems evident that a teacher exploring the contemporary world of science and space travel with students would find Franklyn M. Branley's *Experiments in the Principles of Space Travel, A Book of Moon Rockets for You,* and *Exploring by Astronaut: The Story of Project Mercury* especially interesting. Likewise, Michael Chester's and David McClinton's *The Moon: Target for Apollo,* David Dietz's *All About Satellites and Space Ships,* Theodore W. Munch's *What is a Rocket,* George Gamow's *The Moon,* S. Carl Hirsch's *The Globe for the Space Age,* Jack Coggins' and Fletcher Pratt's *Rockets, Satellites and Space Travel,* and J. A. Hynek's *Challenge of the Universe* would add accurate contemporary information, depth, various reading levels, and excitement to any elementary science unit designed to help youngsters become more aware of our space program.

The list of fine science informational books for a unit on rockets and space is seemingly endless. The content they offer will not be found in most texts. Their development and concern for detail will not be found in current science magazines or in pamphlets. The information is in trade book form—exciting, accurate, and well-written.

## ENRICHMENT

Much has been said and written about the need to enrich the science curriculum. Much needs to be said about the enrichment of the entire curriculum. It is through the enriched curriculum, in all areas, that much of the most valuable learning takes place. The enrichment of a program, such as the science program, implies open-ended learning and a trend toward individualization, both valid learning schemes.

The enrichment of a program means that the learning environment provides, as much as possible, for meeting the individual educational needs of all youngsters. Enrichment implies permission for leaving the often rigid, prescribed course direction and investigating specializations within an area. It implies acceptance of individual ability levels and attempts to assist the more able student to reach greater heights of understanding by permitting and encouraging him to go above and beyond what the unit or course of study prescribes. Enrichment will also permit the less able student to investigate at his own rate an area of interest to him if he is unable to function well with the whole class as it moves toward concepts and generalizations that are beyond his grasp. Enrichment also implies individual investigation, aside from the regular program, for the student who wishes it. The enrichment of a curriculum does exactly what it says it will do: make the learning environment more fertile by providing additional resources and opportunities for learning and allowing time and space for the utilization of these resources in the learning environment.

Any enriched program needs resources other than the basic ones to facilitate its goals. In an enriched learning environment, educational technology operates at its peak level. Some elementary science enrichment resources would likely be mobile laboratories and other devices to encourage experimentation or manipulation, closed circuit television, tape recorders, films, slides, outside resource persons visiting the classroom, field trips and visits to science-oriented businesses and industries or the university science department. Present among the resources to enrich the program should be a wealth of books. Many of the fine text and reference books should be in evidence and available to children. Prominent also among this collection of books for enrichment should be the children's science trade books.

An enriched science environment in an elementary school should have available trade books concerned with many and varied scientific topics. Here the youngster can browse and explore ideas both familiar and new. It is in this collection that he can first meet ideas about radioactivity, bird migration, volcanoes, astronomy, electricity, and the like. These books will provide an educational cafeteria where the student can taste and sample many scientific fares and likely develop a taste for a certain field that can develop into a valuable, long-range interest. Here, too, the young scientist can read the biographies of the famous people of science and learn that they also were people who had a childhood and problems; they, too, will become dimensional and real to the children who will read about them. The inspired lives of Thomas Edison, Madam Curie, Albert Einstein, and George Washington Carver, among others, await the youngsters in the form of children's biographies.

These trade books, geared to enrich the science program, can provide the youngster with additional data and interpretation of data, as well as new ideas. These books can raise questions in the minds of the youngsters so as to act as a genesis for further exploration and investigation. The science trade books can enhance the youngster's concept of what science and inquiry are all about. These books do a fine job of accomplishing what they were designed to do: enrich the child's science experiences.

The children's trade book as an enrichment resource has some valuable intrinsic qualities that often cannot be found in other instructional resources. Unique in the trade book as an enrichment resource are:

1.　These resources are highly portable. They can be taken by the student wherever he wishes to take them. The trade book can accompany the youngster to his home, on vacation, on the bus to school, or just about anywhere the youngster goes.

2.　It can be individually paced by the youngster who uses it. He proceeds in his interaction with it, as he wishes to. He can go as rapidly or as leisurely as he desires. It is always available to him, waiting to be used again where he left off.

3.　It is reusable. It is not a consumable resource, in the usual sense, due to the fact that a youngster can use the book again and again and recommend it to others.

4.　It offers infinite variety. It offers not only variety of content, but variety in presentation, as well. A child's interest in jet aircraft, for instance, can be satisfied and fed by trade books about the topic from a low primary level to an advanced, sophisticated level that would answer most questions an adult would ask.

Enrichment of the curriculum in the elementary school is an educationally sound practice. It is a practice that often increases the learning level of students above their expected achievement. In science education, enrichment practices are almost a necessity, if the youngsters are to be provided with opportunities to explore the natural world. The children's science trade book is prominent among those resources geared to provide enrichment. The value of children's literature as an enrichment resource in an elementary school science program is difficult to overestimate.

## THE SCIENCE ACTIVITY

The science curriculum in the elementary school implies activity. The very nature of the discipline suggests that the learner do something, involve himself physically in the process of learning about science. The enrichment possibilities demand this activity. The adventure of a science unit is exciting, dynamic, and *fun!* As Gerald S. Craig so aptly states,

> . . . science is not merely the job of teaching a child subject matter for his passive acceptance. In addition to understanding, science involves doing, reading, working, thinking, planning, co-operating, and intelligently operating with the natural forces in the classroom, on the school ground, in the community, and in experimenting with simple materials.[3]

If the activity is a game, as in certain mathematical activities, the raising of tadpoles to frogs, maintaining a classroom terrarium, collecting rocks and minerals, working with levers, or the like, the youngster is quite often caught up in the adventure of it and learns from it because it is fascinating and fun. The activity program (some would call an activity program "enrichment" and the author would argue that point) is one of the most successful techniques that the teacher can employ to help children learn from and about science. It is successful because it is active—children are actually involved in firsthand, primary experiences concerning the natural world. Because they are actively involved, the learning becomes immediate and important. The children actually experience the wonders of the universe in a well-planned, carefully executed activity unit in the science program.

---

[3] Gerald S. Craig, *Science for the Elementary School Teacher*, 5th ed. (Waltham, Mass.: Blaisdell Publishing Company, 1966), p. 111.

Any activity program that involves children is bound to generate questions and a need for information.

> "How long before the polliwog becomes a frog?"
>
> "How can we tell the difference between fool's gold and real gold?"
>
> "How many babies will the hamster have?"
>
> "How long will it take for the caterpillar to become a butterfly?"

Questions such as these, and hundreds more like them, are familiar to the teacher who employs an activity program and realia as a regular part of the science program. The curiosity of children seems to work overtime, and thus their learning, too, when they become involved in a science program that involves activity.

The teacher of science knows that sources of information, and lots of them, need to be at hand if the curiosity of children is to be transformed into learning. Here again is a role for the children's science informational book. Here, beside the terrarium, aquarium, the rock collection, the levers, the animal cage, or whatever the device designed to generate the activity and the questions, should be a collection of good children's science trade books to help the children find the answers they want. Their use by the children will give testimony to their validity.

Among the books to enhance and augment the activity program in the classroom may well be those books that are designed for "fun" science activity outside the classroom, as well. These fine books are designed to help move the science program from the school, whenever possible, to the home, the playground, and into the extra-school environment the youngster has. Such fine books as Nelson F. Beeler's *Experiments with a Microscope* and *Experiments in Chemistry*, Elizabeth K. Cooper's *Science in Your Own Backyard*, Herbert S. Zim's *A Guide to Familiar American Insects* and *Birds: A Guide to the Most Familiar American Birds* are among many others of infinite variety that can assist the child in taking his science adventures out of the classroom and into his life outside. The child who has these sources of information available to him, in the form of children's trade books, will use them. The learning they generate may well influence a lifetime.

## CROSS-REFERENCE CHECKING

Information sometimes conflicts. It conflicts because of different sources of data, different circumstances that time has brought about, or errors the author has made in compiling and reporting his data. Information can be at variance in certain cases when the theory or philosophy of the authors conflicts. It can be a startling experience for an adult to find that information does not always agree in the references he examines. For a child to discover this fact, it can be not only startling but confounding and confusing. We expect *the book* to be the "final authority" in most cases. When that "final authority" does not agree with other "final authorities," the young reader is often, quite frankly, at sea. What should he believe, whom should he believe, and where should he go to get the word that speaks the truth?

As teachers of the young, we face the possibility of having youngsters find conflicting evidence or information that does not agree with the sources, and surprisingly often. It not only happens when youngsters seek information in the sciences, but in other fields, as well. When this happens we most often settle the conflict by providing the final word ourselves or by turning to the ever present and most valuable encyclopedia as the final authority. Both practices are valid and work well as a stop-gap technique.

Another technique, and perhaps even more valid than teacher-provided answers or reference to the encyclopedia, is to help the child learn to evaluate the sources of information that are conflicting. Perhaps we can aid him in developing his critical thinking skills by showing him how to evaluate the many sources that he has available to him in the form of trade books. Perhaps we can help him discover that just because something is in print, it is not always valid or that points of view will sometimes change depending on how one interprets data. What valuable learning that would be for him.

In helping youngsters learn to look critically at the information they receive from the many reading sources that are available to them, the teacher can direct the student's attention to two major points that are often overlooked when they interact with a book.

1. What is the copyright date of the book? If one of the conflicting books is several years older than the other, the older book may be less accurate simply because time has elapsed and more information is now available.

2. Who is the author or authors? Are they experts in the field? Was the book written under the direction of an authority in the area? Many times one of the conflicting books comes from a more authoritative source, and therefore the information contained in it has more validity than the other. Many librarians enclose part of the dust jacket that contains this information. Most often, however, in informational books the author's credentials are included on the title page.

If youngsters become aware of these two variables in evaluating a book, and make use of them, the conflict in information is often resolved.

It is often not enough to have many sources available to the youngster to help him learn. We also need to help him know how to use the sources that are available to him. To critically examine a book, to look at the sources that produced the book, to be aware of the age of the book and the information it contains, is a valuable step toward scholarship. The research and cross-reference checking that children do in the science program, as well as in other areas of the curriculum, will many times produce valuable learning that seems secondary to the problem being solved but actually may be of equal importance. In seeking answers, the student often discovers as much from learning how to seek as he does from finding the answer that started his search.

## THE SCIENCE HOBBY

One of the most pressing problems our society will face in the next decade will be how to spend its leisure time. Technology, we

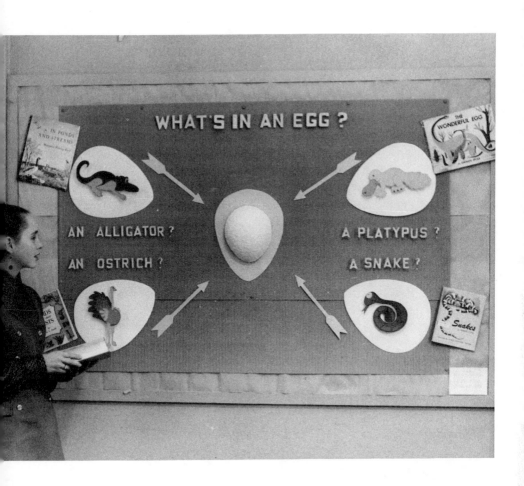

The enrichment of a science activity is heightened by the use of good children's literature. The science information books featured here need to be available for children's immediate use.

When a child discovers a good book he will often
recommend it to others. This is one of the most effective
ways that literature for children can become a
regular, important part of their lives.

*School setting: Lincoln Elementary School, Stockton, California*
PHOTO: APERTURE LIMITED, STOCKTON, CALIFORNIA

are told, will relieve the need for many of the current manpower hours now expended in work activities. By the year 2000, the workweek for the average American will be much less than it is currently. Some tell us that because of technology, work activity of certain kinds will not exist. The adult of the year 2000 will have many hours of leisure time available to him. How he spends it will be of concern to his entire culture.

The teacher working with today's child is concerned about the adult the child will become and about the emerging world that child will occupy. As teachers, we are very concerned about the academic and social preparation our students receive to get them ready for adult life in the emerging world. We are greatly concerned about developing positive skills and controls, concepts and generalizations, attitudes and behavior patterns in our students that will aid them in later life. These are, after all, the warp and woof of teaching.

Perhaps, in light of the prognosis that tells us about the emerging world of the year 2000, we, as teachers, need to be equally concerned with the task of helping our students learn to use leisure time more wisely. If what we are told about the future of society and the role of technology in it is true, we are not preparing our students adequately for life in that future society. Perhaps the curriculum itself needs to provide for such learning.

One step that we, as educators of the young, can take in helping students develop attitudes about how to use leisure time wisely is to provide a genesis for positive out-of-school activity in our classrooms. We can provide, in school, the motivation and the tools that may spark the interest of a youngster and cause him to take his interest and activity from the classroom into his life away from school. We can, in short, provide the setting for the development of hobbies and interests that can serve the student well by giving him hours of productive, interesting activity and perhaps the start of a life-long interest that will provide worthy use of leisure time for years to come.

The science curriculum in the elementary school is, of course, a "natural" for this kind of activity. Children are fascinated with the world and all it contains. They are enchanted with animal life and all the secrets that nature holds for those who will seek. They ponder the physical sciences and are amazed at the energy the natural world holds in reserve. The mysteries and beauties a well-developed science program has will hold the attention and the imagination of youngsters as a magnet holds metal. To generate enough interest in the science curriculum to take it beyond the school environment and into the personal life of a student, is a remarkably simple task. The science hobby is a natural outgrowth of many science units.

One of the most common, and certainly one of the most successful, science units in the elementary school is the study of geology. This unit, concerned with the earth's crust and the many manifestations it offers in terms of rocks and minerals, opens a new world of thought and process to youngsters. The study of volcanoes, glaciers, magma, conditions below the earth's surface, mountain building, and the like, has drama and excitement that can favorably compare with any thriller playing at the theatre on Saturday afternoon. To help children become aware of the fact that certain rocks and minerals are available for collection by simply looking about on the ground, in the backyard, or in the vacant lot, may start them to compare, classify, and collect these pebbles. If this happens, the genesis of a science hobby has likely begun. The wise teacher will provide opportunities for youngsters to trade samples and visit a rock store or hobby shop where rock and mineral specimens are available. The teacher will introduce the youngsters to lapidary and perhaps provide a demonstration for them in the art and process of stonecutting and polishing. The teacher can provide names and addresses of other rock and mineral "hounds" throughout the country (easily obtained from most rock and mineral hobby magazines) so that trading and comparing notes can develop through the mails. Of course, classroom time needs to be provided for this activity during the science period. Rock and mineral collections will grow and they will travel between home and school. They may provide the genesis for a hobby that may continue for many years.

As the science hobby develops, more and more need for specific information becomes apparent. Children engaged in a hobby find themselves deeply involved, and the more time spent in the pursuit of the hobby, the greater the involvement becomes. Information of a rather specific nature is sought. The texts are soon exhausted. The children's informational trade book is the source that children will turn to next, if they are available to them. These books will be read, examined, discussed, shared, and read again for the information they hold. The wealth of information they contain will most always match the need the hobbyist has for information. The circulation of these books is guaranteed. We, as teachers, must make them a part of our classroom library collection.

Whatever the science hobby, there are many fine informational books available to satisfy the need of the hobbyist.* From atoms to zoology, from ants to zinc, informational trade books are available to enhance and undergird the science hobby. For a unit on rocks and minerals, for example, the teacher can quickly find such fine trade books as W. M. Reed's *The Earth for Sam*, B. John Syrocki's *What is a Rock*, Herbert S. Zim's *Rocks and Minerals: A Guide to Familiar Minerals, Gems, Ores and Rocks*, Patricia Lauber's *The Changing Face of North America*, and Anne T. White's *All About Our Changing Rocks* among many others. A search in the library, or a talk with the children's librarian, will uncover enough books on the topic to satisfy the most questioning hobbyist.

Developing attitudes about and providing for positive leisure-time activity, such as the hobby, may well be a necessary part of the elementary school curriculum. The science hobby, one of the most easily developed out-of-school activities that have their genesis in the classroom, may well be a goal that science teachers strive for. The science hobby develops a need for additional information outside the text and regular reference sources. Children's literature, in the form of science informational trade books, is certainly one source to provide that needed information.

## Summary

CHILDREN'S LITERATURE CAN PLAY an important role in undergirding and enhancing the elementary science program. In an age that

---

* See the suggested science bibliographies at the end of this chapter.

is scientific, and in a time when the information explosion is expanding at so rapid a rate, the student of science can no longer depend upon his primary experiences and his science text to give him the information he needs. He must go beyond the standard material available to him to begin to grasp the vastness of the field. The children's trade book is an invaluable tool that can help him expand his scientific knowledge.

The children's trade book, particularly the informational book, can help the young student of science to keep abreast of the new developments that occur with amazing regularity. Certainly, the trade book's ability to deepen and extend concepts that are offered a student in the science program make these books a necessary and valuable part of his scientific environment.

The skills of research and experimentation are also enhanced when a rich collection of scientific trade books is available to the youngster. He is able to use these fine books for cross-reference checking, for enrichment exercises, and for confirmation of conflicting evidence. Many teachers find the scientific trade book essential when these skills are developed in the elementary science unit.

The science hobby, so important in developing the young scientist as well as providing for a worthy use of leisure time, is often augmented by the use of children's scientific literature. The hobbyist's need for additional and specialized information can many times be satisfied through interacting with a varied collection of good children's books.

The science trade books available to youngsters cover a vast field of content, depth, and interest. The elementary teacher of science who ignores these fine materials is doing herself and her students a grave injustice.

# EXERCISES
## FOR THE TEACHER

1.　Examine several elementary science texts. Note their publication date. Note their content. How long before the book was published, was it written? How long ago was it published?

2.　At the children's room in the public library or at the library in an elementary school or school district office, note the trade books that deal with scientific concepts. Make a list of the range of topics.

3.　Prepare a bulletin board using the dust jackets from trade books about science. Design the bulletin board to feature one unit of study or one concept in elementary school science.

4.　Find a science unit in an elementary science text. How can this unit be deepened and enhanced by carefully selected children's trade books dealing with the same information?

5.　Interview a youngster who has a science hobby or who has a deep interest in a branch of science. Ask what books he reads. How many of them are trade books?

6.　Prepare a "book talk" featuring one science trade book.

7.　In the biography section of the children's collection, how many biographies are about famous scientists?

8.　In an informational science book, note the illustrations. Can a slow reader get scientific information from this book? How?

9.　What science phenomena in the average home (pets, television, telephone, electricity, heat, etc.) can be better understood by the use of good science literature? What books are available to build that better understanding?

10. What role does science fiction play in the elementary science program?

11. Compile a bibliography of children's trade books that will undergird a science unit that you are planning.

12. Does your local library have additional bibliographies other than those listed for science books in this text?

13. Interview a science education specialist. How does he see the role of children's literature in the science program?

14. Examine the reading materials from such programs as The Elementary Science Study and The Minnesota Mathematics and Science Project. Are these trade materials? How can they be enhanced by the use of trade books?

# SUGGESTED READINGS

AMERICAN ASSOCIATION FOR THE ADVANCEMENT OF SCIENCE. *Science.* Washington, D. C.: American Association for the Advancement of Science, weekly.

_____. Science Book List. Washington, D. C.: American Association for the Advancement of Science, 1959.

_____. *Science Book List for Young Adults.* Washington, D. C.: American Association for the Advancement of Science, 1964.

BLOUGH, GLENN O., and HUGGETT, ALBERT J. *Elementary School Science and How to Teach It.* New York: The Dryden Press, 1953.

COUNCIL OF CHIEF STATE SCHOOL OFFICERS. *A Consolidated, Classified, and Annotated List of Recommended Books on Science, Mathematics and Foreign Languages.* Hillside, N. J.: Baker and Taylor, 1963.

CRAIG, GERALD S. *Science for the Elementary School Teacher.* 5th ed. Waltham, Mass.: Blaisdell Publishing Company, 1966.

DEASON, HILARY. *Science Book List for Children.* Washington, D. C.: American Association for the Advancement of Science, 1963.

*Growing Up with Science Books.* New York: R. R. Bowker Company, Annual.

HAMAN, ALBERT C., and EAKIN, MARY. *Library Material for Elementary Science: An Educational Service Publication.* Cedar Falls: State College of Iowa, 1964.

RENNER, JOHN W., and RAGAN, WILLIAM B. *Teaching Science in the Elementary School.* New York: Harper and Row Publishers, 1968.

ROBINSON, EVELYN, ed. *Reading About Children's Literature*, Part IX. New York: David McKay Company, Inc., 1966.

TANNENBAUM, HAROLD E., STILLMAN, NATHAN, and PILTZ, ALBERT. *Science Education for Elementary School Teachers.* 2nd ed. Boston: Allyn and Bacon, Inc., 1965.

*Chapter IV*

# CHILDREN'S LITERATURE
# AND THE ARTS

*A dichotomy, of sorts,*
exists between the arts. In our specialized society one might expect
this. The arts are separated by some into the plastic arts, the arts
of movement and dance, the musical arts, and the language arts,
among others. They all deal with the phenomenon of creation; of
reorganizing, reshaping and redefining that which exists into a
new, novel, and hopefully, better product. Art implies beauty,
be it in plastic, language, or dance form. Art signifies our species'
finest moments. It is one important factor that separates man from
the lower animals, in that the arts can only be practiced by man.
The arts manifest the yearnings, the thoughts, the ideals, and the
aesthetic needs of man's adventure on earth. He who would
practice the arts has long been considered a special person. The
Greeks, in fact, thought of the artist as a favorite of the gods.

The dichotomy that exists between the arts is perhaps a necessary thing. No one person has ever mastered all of them. The
painter concentrates on and develops his art as a way of com-

municating to the world his thoughts and ideas. The composer of music uses his medium to do the same. The artist who uses language toils long and hard to find words, phrases, sentences, and paragraphs that will correctly and beautifully convey what he feels needs to be conveyed. The artist often needs to channel his efforts in one area, with one medium, if he is to become proficient and skillful in his art. Thus, we have one major reason for the dichotomy among the arts.

As teachers of children, we are, of course, aware of the budding talents of our students. We watch with proud amazement as a creative, gifted child responds to the environment we have provided and produces a fine piece of work. Talent is a commodity that we admire and need to nurture. Creativity is a quality we all possess but the youngster with a high degree of this special quality is a rare and valuable person in our classroom setting. The dichotomy between the arts is apparent when the talented child finds a medium that facilitates his need to create. He will pursue his art through this medium, often to the exclusion of others. Real creative talent is often apparent in elementary school children. One of our jobs as teachers is to encourage it.

The classroom setting is an important environment in the nurturing of the artistic and creative child. We, as teachers, need to provide stimulus in our classrooms for the development of all the arts. Not all children will or can become practicing artists. All children, however, can become consumers of art. The experiences they have with the arts in our classrooms can develop attitudes and appreciations that can well affect them during their lifetime.

Children's literature can play an important role in helping children develop a sensitive, receptive attitude toward the arts. Because of the nature of children's trade books, the language and plastic arts of illustration are the most obvious features that a children's book holds for artistic education. Children's trade books are after all a combination of words and illustrations in juxtaposition, whose final results are meant to give pleasure, information, ideas, and beauty. Few educational resources can help children understand and appreciate the art of language and illustration better than good children's literature.

## EXPOSING CHILDREN TO THE BEST WRITING
## IN OUR LANGUAGE

Most language experts agree that language is learned in an imitative manner. Children hear a language as part of their early environment and take the language, through imitation, as one of their functioning life tools. Language patterns, dialect and linguistic sets are usually well defined by the time a youngster enters school. He can usually understand his language and can communicate certain wants and ideas by using his oral language. The school then sets about building upon the language facilities the youngster has, and attempts to improve and enhance his language so that he can communicate in his culture in an effective, productive way. Much of his language learning is done outside of school but an important part of that learning is done in the school environment.

Much of the language learning that is done in the elementary school is done by hearing and seeing models of language. The teacher is certainly a most important language model. A teacher is a communicator and she communicates with language a large part of the time. She sets a standard for language. Children listen to her and read what she presents to them. They listen, speak, read, and write using the vocabulary they have. The teacher, using her professional skills and acting as a language model, extends their vocabulary and facility with language.

Children's literature is an invaluable resource to the teacher who wishes to extend language and language experiences. Children in the early primary grades eagerly listen when a good book is read and enjoy the experience of prose in one of its finest forms. By listening they can become acquainted with the concept of words used as an artist uses them, in a way that can truly be called a "language art." The beauty of language is a necessary part of good children's literature. In these fine books, words touch the imagination of children. They listen and want to listen again. Words are used in new and exciting ways. New words or words that are unfamiliar take on meaning when in the context of a good story. Words become more than just letters on a page—they are funny, sad, happy, or quiet—depending upon the book and its content. For many children the first beautiful language they ever hear comes to them from the pages of a good children's trade book. The language used in children's literature is a vital language experience for young children.

Children in the middle and upper grades, as well, enjoy and learn from having books read orally to them. They want to enjoy books read to them that go beyond their level of reading comprehension but which are of interest to them and to their age group. They need and want to experience the magic of the beautiful language that is found in so many fine children's trade books. Children in the middle and upper grades will often remark on "how it was said" or "you can almost see it when he describes it" when interacting with a trade book. The awareness of the power of language is beginning to form when youngsters remark about how an author uses words in telling his story. Language is seen as an art.

Experience with good prose writing, either as he hears it read by the teacher or as he reads it himself in a book of his own choosing, is a vital part of developing the concept that language can be an art. Much of what children read during a busy school year is for information and direction. This is necessary and good. This kind of reading should be balanced, however, with literature that is evocative, imaginative, well constructed and full of descriptive language. Language, indeed, can be an art. Children must be helped to realize this and appreciate it. One of the most effective ways of bringing this awareness to children is by providing them with a rich environment of good prose in children's trade books.

The trade book, used as a model for art in language, both on the primary and upper grade level, needs to be fine literature. It needs to offer children an opportunity to experience the very best writing in our language. It needs to offer a good plot, a psychological level in which children will better understand themselves and others as a result of experiencing the book, and when possible, a symbolic level, a theme or message that transcends the story and represents a large or universal truth. Most important, however, is the language used. A great children's book, like a great book for the adult, depends upon the language used in telling the story. We have every right to expect the same artistry in language in books for children as we do in books for adults. When we stop expecting it, literature for children will become less than it should be.

In choosing the books for children that will serve as a model for art in language, we, as teachers, face a formidable, yet delightful task. Not all books for children contain the elements that make for literary excellence. As in adult literature, much is available that can be termed "pure junk." Happily, amid the junk, the jewels glow with clear brightness. For the uninitiated, however, finding them can be a problem. For the teacher who will seek literature for children that will provide experience with the finest writing in our language and serve as a model for language use and learning, help is readily available.

The teacher might:

1.  Contact the children's librarian employed by the school district or at the public library and tell her of the needs and ask for suggestions. The children's librarian is a primary source that should be used again and again.

2.  Consult one or more of the better texts concerning children's literature as a literary form. Such fine books as May Hill Arbuthnot's *Children and Books*, Lillian Hollowell's *A Book of Children's Literature*, Nancy Larrick's *Teacher's Guide to Children's Books*, among others, will acquaint the teacher with some of the finest children's books available.

3.  Read the books you have chosen before bringing them to children as a model for art in language. The experts may all agree that a certain children's book is a masterpiece, and it probably is. But, it may not be *the* book for your class at *this* time to serve as a language model. It is good to read the book before it is used.

An educational environment that will foster language learning needs to be rich in the use of language. Models for language need to be excellent and easily available to the student whose language we seek to extend and enhance. The art of language as found in good children's literature can be found in few other sources. As a resource in language learning, the children's trade book has few peers.

## DEVELOPING TASTE
## IN CHILDREN'S LITERATURE

One of the major purposes of teaching literature in the elementary schools is to help children develop successively higher levels of appreciation and tastes in the selection of their reading material. This aim has been reiterated in the writing of educational authorities for years ...[1]

Indeed, if we are teaching children to read so that they will become readers of books, not just those who can read, we, as teachers, need to be concerned about *what* they read and the *quality* of literature they read. Concern is also needed to help children upgrade their taste in literature. Appreciation for the art of literature should be a goal of teachers from kindergarten through graduate school. The foundations for this appreciation is built in large part by the literary environment provided in the elementary school. The elementary classroom is the cornerstone in the edifice of literary appreciation. The attitudes toward the art of literature start in the young child. It is difficult to change it in adolescence or during the years of adulthood.

Research concerning the development of taste in literature is admittedly sparce. The concern of research seems to be to find out how much children read rather than the quality of what they read. The research that has been done, however, does give us some clues as to how we, as teachers, can upgrade the literary fare our children will choose to read.

The studies reviewed reveal several constant threads in the development of taste in children's reading. They are not surprising, but may serve to strengthen that which good teachers already know and practice. If we are to improve the taste of children in selecting and interacting with children's literature, the classroom environment we provide should contain the following:

1. An enthusiastic, competent teacher, who is familiar with good children's literature and employs good teaching techniques.

---

[1] National Conference on Research in English, *Development of Taste in Literature* (Champaign, Ill.: The National Council of Teachers of English, 1963), p. 8.

2. A supply of good, carefully selected children's books available to children in the classroom and an opportunity to interact with them.

3. Library activity as a regular part of the classroom program. Frequent visits to the school or public library should be considered a regular part of the curriculum.

4. A unified arts approach to literature. Literature can be considered an art form along with music and the plastic arts. The approach can be one of enhancing appreciation.

5. Lots of the best in children's literature. Call attention to specific books for specific children. An attractive display featuring the books available will draw attention to the offering.

6. Discussion of the books that are available in the classroom collection. Share children's comments about the books with their classmates. "Book talks" by the teacher and children create an interest and will whet the appetite for the better selections.

7. Oral reading by the teacher of the better books will help to create a need for high quality. Youngsters appreciate what is good and will not be satisfied with less, once they have been exposed to the best. Oral reading by the teacher is a good way to present "the best" to an entire class.

8. Utilize creative writing as a way of helping children recognize and appreciate the art of writing. Encourage them to examine the work of a fine author and notice how he has used the artistry of words.

Literary taste is a personal thing. Not all children will like all books, even if they are all well written. Improvement of literary taste should not imply that all children will like a certain list of books, or that one or two pieces of literature, favorites of the teacher perhaps, should be read by all students. The contrary is true. The subject, style, approach, length, level of sophistication and the format of a children's trade book is subject to a variation of acceptance by youngsters. The world of children's literature can comfortably meet all personal requirements of youngsters and still remain within the realm of good literature. When a literary environment demands that all children conform to a list of required reading, the joy of reading will cease. Conformity is dangerous in and by itself in a classroom setting. In an environment meant to enhance children's taste in literary fare, it can be disastrous.

Sometimes, as teachers, we become overly concerned about the material our students read. Sometimes in our lack of understanding about children and their developing reading habits and tastes, we revert to a forced conformity in our classrooms in the hope that this forced conformity will yield the results we so much want evidenced. That hope is a naive one. The best we can hope for with the required lists, the numbers of books to be read, and the like, is rejection on the part of our clients, the children.

The writer is reminded of a teacher, who, in an honest attempt to improve the literary taste of her students, required that the students in her sixth grade class read a certain number of the Newbery Medal Book winners. She placed a reward, in the form of a grade, on the number of Newbery award winners read during the semester. The more one read, the higher the grade. Perhaps she would have been more realistic if she would have admitted her program produced a result that was closer to: the more they *seemed* to read, the higher the grade. The program encouraged children to be dishonest to achieve a goal.

The intent to improve taste in literature resulted in something quite different. The slavish dependence on the Newbery list for quality was a result of little knowledge of children's literature. Many Newbery award winning books are too advanced for sixth graders, and, besides, many of these books are thought to be deadly dull by children.

The comments above are not meant to belittle the Newbery Medal, or what it represents. These award-winning books are excellent. To conclude that these are the only excellent books for children, however, is very wrong. Many of the most enduring of the children's selections have not won that award. Some of the finest children's literary offerings are not listed on a roster of that kind. The practice of a slavish devotion to a book list of that nature only proved the validity of the old cliché, "a little knowledge is a dangerous thing."

Children sometimes seem to prefer "the junk!" There is a reason why *Nancy Drew* and *Judy Bolton* have lasted as long as they have. The series books, the toy books that squeek, roll on wheels and come complete with pop-up scenery, or the gimmick books that feature lollipops (*Lolly, the Lollipop Girl*) or Band-Aids (*Dr. Dan the Band-Aid Man*) and the like on their shiny plastic covers, do have appeal. They are sold on a mass basis, are quite inexpensive, and are very easy to read. Their appeal is closely related to that of the comics. Children seem to go through a period when these books meet their reading needs. The toy and gimmick books do offer diversion, of a sort, but offer little, if any, literary pleasure. Of course, these books aren't books at all . . . they are toys. They really are not meant to be read at all. They are playthings, cleverly disguised in book form. Many times the series books are read for group reasons. Reading them becomes the accepted, stylish thing to do in many middle grade classroom social climates. The seemingly endless supply of Nancy Drew books, Mark Tidd adventures, the Tom Swift stories, etc. are traded among youngsters and become somewhat status. These books also offer an outlet for the collection urge so apparent in many middle grade youngsters. They are marketed as sets and are easily and in-expensively acquired as collections.

That these books lack real literary quality is obvious. That we, as teachers, should encourage our students to seek literature with a higher degree of literary value is also obvious. Yet, how can we encourage children to leave junk material and move into more re-warding books?

Book banning is certainly not the answer. One sure way to foster the popularity of these books is to forbid their being read. Publishers of adult novels know the value of having a book banned. It will assure soaring sales and considerable monetary returns. Some publishers actually survive by publishing banned books. If we forbid these books in our classrooms, we very probably will encourage their popularity. The immediate question that many children will probably ask might be: "What's in them that I shouldn't read?" and go busily about finding out what is supposed to be objectionable.

These books will be read by some of our children. Youngsters certainly will not be harmed by them. If the children bring them into the classroom, let them come in. Our attitude toward these books is an important factor in their status among the children. Certainly, we will not feature these books or bring them ourselves into the classroom. Perhaps a somewhat "obvious patience" is one way to react to them when they come into the classroom. Perhaps a somewhat indulgent attitude is best. Children soon get the message.

A bright young man, a teacher in a fifth grade class, recently demonstrated just how this can be done. The youngsters in his classroom, particularly the girls, were off and running with the Nancy Drew mysteries. They blossomed out of lunch baskets, were in desks, were traded and shared. Mr. Tom Howard, the teacher, seemed to ignore the whole Nancy Drew operation. The classroom had a very fine and changing collection of good trade books. He read to the class daily and the children eagerly awaited each new chapter every day. Charlotte was weaving her magic in E. B. White's delightful *Charlotte's Web*. The class and the teacher were enchanted as Wilbur, Charlotte, Templeton and all the barnyard creatures of this great book acted out their adventures, as Mr. Howard read.

When *Charlotte's Web* reached its final conclusion, the usual hush of regret that the book was finished filled the room. White's artistry as an author had worked its charm again. The youngsters hated to leave the characters of the book, as they had become dimensional, real, understandable friends. The book would be read again and again by many children, as the story is just too good for one reading.

Mr. Howard and the class discussed *Charlotte's Web*, talked about White and his writing. He mentioned *Stuart Little*, another children's book by White, and offered it to any who would want it. The class, of course, wanted to know what the next book for oral reading would be. Mr. Howard asked for suggestions. The first hand that went up belonged to Jennifer, a bright-eyed young lady of ten. "Would you," she asked, "read us a Nancy Drew?"

Mr. Howard paused for a moment and then grinned, "Nancy Drew? Are you still interested in those books? I thought fifth graders had outgrown them." The class and Mr. Howard laughed good naturedly and other suggestions were made about the next book to be read aloud.

With that one, good natured, somewhat surprised and indulgent remark, Nancy Drew sailed off into a colorless sunset. I suspect her popularity waned considerably thereafter.

Developing taste in literature is an important part of helping children understand and appreciate the art of language. If we are to help children develop literary taste, we must surround them with the best children's literature available and encourage them to read it. The model the youngster uses as a criterion for excellence in literature is a factor over which we, as teachers, can exercise some control. The literary environment in the classroom is our creation. A literary environment is a major factor in helping children develop good literary taste.

## THE ART OF ILLUSTRATION

In children's literature, illustration is often as important as the text. Many children's books, written for the preschooler or the primary-age child, contains little or no text at all in that the story is to be read by pictures. Many others come to children as a twice-told tale, a tale that is told in text and illustration, both elements supportive of the other. Even literature for older children and the early adolescent contains illustrations that enhance the story. Arbuthnot classifies children's illustrated literature into three categories:

1. The picture book, with little or no text. (Bruno Munari's *ABC*)

2. The picture-story book, a twice-told tale; a tale that is told once in text and once in illustration. (Yashima's *Crow Boy*)

3. The illustrated book, with fewer pictures, but with those that give additional insight into the characters and the setting. (Garth Williams' illustrations in E. B. White's *Charlotte's Web*)[2]

---

[2] May Hill Arbuthnot, *Children and Books*, 3rd ed., p. 52. Copyright 1964 by Scott, Foresman and Co., Chicago.

Regardless of the categories that we may create, children's literature and the art of illustration are inseparable. Combining the talents of the author and the illustrator in creating a book has given us a new form of literature, the wonderful world of children's literature.

Illustrations have been a part of children's books for many years. Only in recent years has the illustrator been allowed to reach the height of an artist. With modern technology and the wide use of the offset printing technique, illustrators of children's books have been given the freedom to truly create. Color, framing, design, and detail no longer present a problem to the illustrator. He can use the pages of a children's book as freely as he uses his canvas. The results have produced a renaissance for children's illustrators and an unbelievable treasure trove of good art available to children.

The illustrator is a communicator. He, too, tells the story. He tells it in a medium different from the author, but his storytelling is every bit as real. He may tell his story with the whimsy of abstractions, the fancy of collage, with brilliant watercolors, pastels, and the realism born from oils. He may tell his story with line drawings, woodblocks, or a myriad of other techniques. Children are all the richer by experiencing the creative use of many techniques to tell a story.

Children will look and look again at the illustrations in a children's book. They will examine the work of a good illustrator and derive real pleasure and literary depth from his efforts. They experience new ways of seeing a city, a pet, a tree, a stream, other people, and the world around them when they examine illustrations in a children's book. They eagerly accept what the artist has to say. They understand the work of the artist as it should be understood: as a way of communicating.

If we, as educators, are sincere in our concern about educating the whole child, then we have a responsibility to educate his aesthetic self, too. We have a responsibility to help the youngster develop as much of his creative sensitivity as possible. We want him to learn to appreciate and understand the work of the artist.

It is often difficult, if not impossible, to bring children and original pieces of art together. Other than field trips to the art museum, or to a local art show, children are often not exposed to good art. The mass media of magazines and newspapers are not greatly concerned, usually, with the level of art that is reproduced in their publications and, of course, the commercial artist is the one who is concerned about the effect his work will have on the sale of a commodity, rather than for its intrinsic value.

Even if youngsters do have an opportunity to visit art museums and exhibits, many times they are not able to grasp what is being made available to them. The foreign environment of the museum is not as conducive to thoughtful viewing as is the familiar classroom. Also, the youngsters often lack the background to really understand what they are seeing. Perhaps beginning art education, or at least the part that builds understanding and appreciation, needs to be done on the child's level and not from the point of view of the adult.

The fine and often great art that is reproduced in some children's books may very well serve as a way to begin art appreciation with children. These illustrations were created for children. Their content and message were conceived with children in mind as their audience. The illustrations are couched in the meaningful context of a story, so that the youngster who views them has a background to use as he interprets them. They are not isolated, distant pieces of art, housed in an unfamiliar environment; they are instead pieces of art designed for children, available in a portable, private format, and in a context that will enhance the understanding and sensitivity that the child employs when he sees it. These illustrations serve as excellent models of good art for the child and they do it in terms that he can easily understand and employ.

The teacher who would use the art in children's books to enhance art appreciation needs to help the youngster grow in his ability to see the artist's craft. The teacher needs to direct attention to the illustrations, not only as a way of telling a story, but as a technique and a medium. How do Marsha Brown, Edward Ardizzone, Maurice Sendak, Celestino Piatti, and Lynd Ward tell their stories? Can we recognize their work in other books? Are they all realistic? How are lines and color used? The teacher through the technique of good selection and discussion can sharpen chil-

Even when it rained or stormed he still came trudging along, wrapped in a raincoat made from dried zebra grass.

The illustrations found in many fine children's trade books add an important dimension to the child's aesthetic education. The beautiful work of Taro Yashima as found in his *Crow Boy* is an example of the fine art work found in many selections of good children's literature.

Good children's literature and the opportunity to interact with it provides one of the most effective ways to stimulate creative thinking. How does *Cinderella* really look? Are all trolls alike? Children are able to construct their own images when stimulated by the contents of good literature.

*School setting: Lincoln Elementary School, Stockton, California*
PHOTO: APERTURE LIMITED, STOCKTON, CALIFORNIA

dren's awareness of the art in illustrations for children's books. This awareness is an important step toward helping children become appreciators of art. The models of good art found in children's literature are a good source that should not be ignored if we strive to develop art appreciation in our elementary schools.

## INITIAL INTRODUCTION TO POETRY

For some reason, many teachers approach poetry for children with caution, if not misgivings. Perhaps our own experience with poetry when we were young students has something to do with it. There was a time when poetry was meant to be memorized and analyzed and was considered too esoteric to enjoy. Poetry needed to be obscure to be good. Hidden meanings, lost thought, and "Airy Faerie" had to be present in the poems if they were of any value. We counted meter and the number of verses that had to be memorized. When we recited, our voices and even our dialect changed to what we imagined was stilted "British Drawing Room." Many of us survived this approach in the elementary school but when we reached the secondary school English classes, the last vestige of enjoyment of poetry was shot down when we worried about iambic pentameter more than we enjoyed the poem. Many of us were never helped to enjoy poetry. A goodly number of us were, I suspect, taught to fear it. The result of this teaching is apparent in our approach to poetry in our elementary classrooms.

Poetry is not, or should not be, an esoteric, obscure experience in literature for children. We should not approach it as something that is difficult to understand and fit only for those with an advanced intellect. Poetry is for all. Children respond to it and love it if we present it in a way that will permit them to enjoy it as another form of children's literature.

Poetry for children offers youngsters another experience with the art of language. Here is another way an artist uses words. The child hears words in a different arangement, in a different order from what he is accustomed to in conversation or prose writing. The cadence, the rhyme, the rhythm, the lilt of poetry make words sing. The sound of words and their juxtaposition in a poem create a musical feeling. Poetry appeals to the senses and can put to use what Shakespeare called "the mind's eye" through the delicate and beautiful imagery that a good poem can offer. Poetry for children should be a joyous experience. It should be a time when children can truly experience the genius of art in language. Their exposure to poetry in the elementary school is likely to be their first exposure to it. We, as teachers, owe it to them to make those first experiences as glorious and pleasurable as possible.

Children's poetry books, and there are many handsome volumes available, need to be present in our classroom collections. These poetry anthologies contain good poetry especially geared to children. These poetry collections, by and large, contain selections that have a strong cadence and rhyme and produce vivid imagery with a story line. They contain nonsense poetry, poetry that plays on and with words, seasonal selections and poems that tell a familiar story in poetic form. They are produced to delight children with a literary form of poetry. Most succeed very well.

Poetry, for the most part, should be heard by children before it is read silently by them. The very nature of poetry asks that it be heard. As teachers in the elementary school, we need to read the poetry we want our children to be exposed to, orally, before we offer it to them in print. We need to let the youngsters hear the magic of the poet's words before they read them themselves. Because poetry is in a form different from prose, children often have a difficult time reading it if they have never heard it. Many adults, for that matter, have a difficult time, too. Cadence and rhyme, when incorrectly handled, become a sing-song, pedantic type of elocution. Rather, a poem should flow and the intrinsic quality of rhythm and rhyme subtly let itself be known. The teacher who reads poetry well can help children know that poetry is not a sing-song exercise but an experience with words that sing with their own music.

Children will often request a teacher to read a certain poem over and over again. This is not unlike children's love for certain songs and melodies they want to sing or hear sung again and again. They enjoy the familiar quality of the poem as an old friend. They are delighted by the familiar beauty of it each time they hear it. It is a wise teacher who will read old favories before introducing a new poem.

Record companies have produced fine recordings of poetry read by professionals, and in some cases, by the poet himself. These can be thrilling experiences in poetry for children. A trained professional with a professional's voice and diction reading a familiar poem can add a dimension to the enjoyment of a poem immeasurably. To hear a poet read his own poems on a recording is indeed a miracle of our technological age.

These recordings, however, wax pale beside the oral reading of a poem by a competent teacher. The teacher is there, alive, and personally sharing the art of poetry with her students. Fortunately, most children still regard people in higher esteem than they do machines.

Should children read poetry orally to their classmates? Certainly! Poetry is a language art and is a way of communication. Poetry should be heard and children should be given experience with the oral reading of it. Poetry, however, should not be read "cold" without preparation. Poetry is not of the same genre as prose and does not often lend itself to spontaneous oral reading by children.

If poems are to be shared by children, give them time to prepare them. Let them hear themselves in small groups, or on a tape recorder, before they share their experience with the class. Let them prepare a presentation. Preparation does not need to be long and involved. Oral reading of poetry by children does not need to carry the connotation of a "production" but it is often unfair to ask a child to read something he is not familiar with and to share it orally with the class.

Shall we require children to memorize poems so that they can have certain poems in their personal repertory? No, I don't think so. A poem, like a song, will become a part of a child if he likes it and wants to keep it. In a good literary environment, where poetry is ever present, children will memorize that which they want to keep. Coercing them into memorizing what we think they should memorize will certainly have a negative effect on the youngster's attitude toward poetry.

Children who have a rich experience with poetry often like

to write poetry themselves. Creative writing is always a delightful time in the school day. It is a time when the children themselves try to create art with language. The models of language we spoke of earlier in this chapter need to be present when a youngster tries his hand at writing poetry, too. He needs to have a good background in poetry before he tries to create a poem himself. The many fine volumes of poetry for children offer him a background which will stand to serve as models of poetry for him. For a novice to work in the medium of an artist will, many times, produce additional respect and admiration for the artist and the art. The youngster who writes his own poems and derives pleasure from doing so will see the art of the poet with a broader and more appreciative eye. That is a major objective of a poetry program in our elementary schools.

## THE ART OF THE PLAYWRIGHT

The youngster who receives the gift of reading from his school should be encouraged to use that gift in all ways to explore the beauty, utility, and versatility of our language. He reads for information and for pleasure. He reads prose and poetry. He learns his language better from his interaction with books, both text and trade. These books serve as a model of language for his growth in language.

The playwright is another artist who uses language effectively in yet another form. The playwright uses language in a dramatic form to communicate his ideas. The script is the technique he employs to tell his story.

It is a rare occurrence when a language or reading text will offer a good script to children. The whole issue of the script and drama seems to have been neglected by the authors of some of our better textbooks. The result, of course, is that children have little opportunity to interact with this form of literature. With drama via television and motion pictures, which is a large part of the youngster's environment, this omission seems to be a glaring one.

There are fine trade books available to the teacher who wishes to introduce the art of the playwright to youngsters. Many publishing companies have produced handsome volumes of scripts for children. One company, Plays, Inc. of Boston, Massachusetts, produces nothing but trade books of and about drama for children. This company, among others, has trade books available about puppetry, play production, tape recorded plays, and the like. It also offers several collections of scripts for both silent and oral reading. The quality of this material is generally very good.

This form of literature is usually very well received by children. They enjoy putting on a play, even if the play is just an oral reading of the script in the classroom. The simple employment of a tape recorder and some sound effects can take a short unit on script reading to the level of a Broadway opening for the children involved. Puppet theatre, puppet making, and a good script can take the language arts to great heights in an elementary classroom. A good collection of scripts, in any one of the many volumes available, will also serve as a model for those children who wish to create their own dramatic literature.

The dramatic form is another way to use art in language. It is yet another place where children's literature can serve the curriculum in a creative way.

## CHILDREN'S LITERATURE
## AND CREATIVE DRAMA

Watching children at play is a delight! The magic carpet of youthful imagination can turn an ordinary playground or classroom into Fort Apache, Cinderella's kitchen, or the sewing room preparing the Emperor's new clothes with a flick of the eye. Sandpiles become superhighways, brooms become horses, tables become giant airfields, or toy blocks are transformed into skyscrapers under the management of young creative minds. Imaginative, dramatic play is a natural part of being young. Pretending at play is a part of human maturation.

Industry has long recognized that fantasy, or the world of

make-believe, is an integral part of childhood. Entire business enterprises are built on this premise. We need only to look at the local department store, the supermarket, the drugstore, or the five-and-ten to see how business flourishes on the need for creative, dramatic play. Toy holsters, Indian regalia, dolls, trucks and cars have proven over the years to be lucrative, indeed.

That this natural part of childhood, the act of pretending at play, should become an integral part of a classroom's educational activity, is becoming more and more obvious to educators. It is a teaching tool that should not be overlooked.

Children's literature has been a traditional source of stories for creative drama. Selections from the folktales, the classics and contemporary children's literature all serve as excellent vehicles for dramatic play. This kind of creative drama is probably the most widely used in the classroom. Its relative ease of execution and natural manifestation has made it a long-time favorite of creative teachers. The skillful use of this technique can add a dimension to literary understanding and provide usage for the language skills rarely found in other approaches.

Children sharing a story, read orally, or in storytelling form, and the subsequent preparation for dramatization is an excellent way of experiencing and examining a good story. Few techniques are better for enhancement of literature appreciation. The discussion of characters, motivation, setting, time and emotional content can transcend the simple reading or hearing of a story and can become an empathic, dynamic literary experience. The use of creative dramatics with children's literature can bring print into vivid, physical life. The encouragement of creative, imaginative thinking necessary in the preparation of creative drama can result in helping children realize the magic and potential of the printed word. Dramatic play requires mutual creative effort between the author and his audience (an important step in the appreciation of literature) if the play is to be satisfying and successful. An experience with creative drama can start a whole new attitudinal syndrome on the part of the reader or listener. The discovery that interpretation of characters, themes, and motivations within a given story can vary according to the receiver, is a major step in developing literary awareness and sensitivity.

The steps in creating a dramatic play situation with children's literature have been outlined by Dewey Chambers and Burdette Fitzgerald.

These steps are:

1.   Tell (or read) the story. A story with high action and few well-defined characters is best.

2.   Discuss the story with the children in detail. Examine characters, setting, motivation of activity carefully. Determine how the characters look, what kind of clothing they should wear, what the setting is like, why they behave the way they do. Break the story down into "acts" with the children. Choose one scene for the play. Examine the scene for sequence of action, setting, and characters.

3.   Cast the characters. This should be done with help from the children. Let them know others will have a chance to play the characters when the story is replayed.

4.   Play the scene. Allow the players a few minutes to consult before they start. Direct the remaining class to watch the play and remember five (more or less) things they liked about the play and five things they would improve when it is played again. Start the play with a signal that is understood by the entire group.

5.   When the play has been completed, stop the action and evaluate the play. Ask the audience for the points they noted (step 4). Make sure the positive as well as the negative points are expressed. Offer your evaluation as well.

6.   Recast and replay the scene. It is important that the steps, outlined above, be followed again. This often spells the difference between success and failure with this technique.[3, 4]

The teacher needs to remember that dramatic play or creative drama is not theatre for children. There are no scripts, settings, costumes. The entire play period depends upon creative, imaginative,

---

[3] Dewey Chambers, *Literature for Children: Storytelling and Creative Drama* (Dubuque, Iowa: Wm. C. Brown Co., 1970).

[4] Burdette Fitzgerald, *Let's Act the Story* (Palo Alto, Calif.: The Fearon Press, 1957).

spontaneous play. The value lies in the process, not the final result, although the final result should be a satisfying experience for the children.

Long involved action in a story is often difficult for children to play. A story or scene should rarely go longer than five minutes for the beginner in a dramatic play. As facility with this technique increases, longer time spans can be used successfully.

Creative drama or dramatic play offers a multitude of opportunities to enhance and develop language skills. The nature of the activity and the skills used in its execution are language skills.

The skills of listening get an opportunity to develop and grow when dramatic play is in the offing. The story must be heard and remembered in detail if the following play session is to be successful. Children know they must listen for sequence of action, character understanding, physical surroundings, and important dialogue if they intend to act out the story.

The skills of oral planning are essential in reconstructing the story for play. The ideas of taking turns, expressing ideas and transforming them into plans for action, enhancing one's own ideas or another's in a planning session are put into practical use. The realization that planning needs to be an orderly, progressive process takes on primary immediacy in a session for organizing dramatic play. The opportunities to experience peer-group planning are difficult to equal when children become involved in an experience of this kind.

The skills of thinking and speaking have an excellent opportunity to develop while "on one's feet." The playing of a character in a creative drama encourages verbal facility. Speaking clearly, and with some dramatic skill, are aspects of this technique that children clearly understand.

Criticism of children, by other children, often becomes a negative, destructive activity. The fact that criticism, if it is to be of value, needs to be constructive is a difficult concept for some children. The idea that criticism does not have to be an act of "finding what is wrong," but can be "finding what is right," is also a new concept for many children. When the group evaluates a play before recasting and replaying, the skills of criticism are put into action. The teacher asks the children to watch the play for aspects of what they *like* and for aspects that need to change when the play is next performed. She encourages the group to note the good points that need to be kept, but also to watch for parts that can be improved by change. By skillful discussion techniques, the teacher can develop valuable attitudes toward criticism when she employs literature-based dramatic plays.

Without a doubt, one of the most important values in this technique is the aspect of opportunities for creativity. Educational research and writing give us a clear picture of the importance of helping the creative, divergent-thinking student develop his potential, as well as providing creative experiences for all students. Teachers know that creativity cannot come from a vacuum. Encouraging creativity and providing opportunities for its flowering is a responsibility all of us must take. Certainly, the technique of creative drama with children's literature will provide rewarding, exciting experiences in creative learning.

## THE ARTS AND NONFICTION LITERATURE FOR CHILDREN

The shelves of the children's library contain a host of trade books about the various arts and artists. They are usually found in the form of biographies or informational books. These books, too, can enhance the child's aesthetic learning by offering a wealth of material to the youngster who is interested in a particular art form or who wants to know more about a great artist. The trade format, along with the specific information these books are able to offer, lends itself well to the needs of children.

From the ballet, Katherine Walker's *Eyes on the Ballet* to pottery, Denys Val Baker's *The Young Potter;* from the theatre, J. B. Priestley's *The Wonderful World of the Theatre* to the biography of Mozart, Opal Wheeler's *Mozart, the Wonder Boy,* these books offer specialized information to the youngster who seeks.

In these books, the young artist can find more about his interest in a particular art and can, in fact, learn about operations and techniques in practicing his art. The student of dance, music, and voice likewise can read about the successful professional in the field and find out more about the world of the artist in his milieu.

For many youngsters, the ballet lessons, the voice lessons, the interest in the theatre, and the music lessons create an interest in the field not unlike that of the hobbyist. His interest often demands more knowledge about the specific art area and his interest is often intense. The nonfiction children's literature can feed his interest, and, in many cases, even help it grow.

## FOLK LITERATURE, OUR LITERARY HERITAGE

The names Buffalo Bill, Rip Van Winkle, Paul Bunyan, John Henry, Sweet Betsy from Pike, Billy the Kid, Joaquin Murietta, Johnny Appleseed, Pecos Bill, Br'er Rabbit, Frebold Freboldson, and the Jumping Frog of Calaveras County tell us of still another literary form: folk literature.

The folktale is one aspect of a larger category, folklore. The folktale refers to the "unwritten" literature of a people, to the tales that have been handed down from generation to generation in the oral tradition. The folktale includes legends, myths, fables, and fairy tales. In its broader sense, it may include folk songs, proverbs, rhymes, and riddles. The folktale, which started in the oral tradition of the storyteller, has since met the printing press, and thus has become frozen in print. The many fine collections of folktales that are available to children are a valuable link connecting them to their literary heritage.

We, in the United States, because of our rich diversity of ethnic groups, reap a harvest of folktales. The immigrants from Central, Northern and Southern Europe brought their folktales with them when they came to our shores. The Negro brought his folktales from Africa, as did the immigrants from the Orient and from Latin America. The result, of course, is a rich mosaic of folktales from all around the world. These tales, coupled with those that were born in the United States, give us a heritage of folk literature that is difficult to equal any place on earth.

This wealth of folktales has resulted in some of the most charming trade books available in the realm of children's literature. The patina of age and use make these tales glow with a special light. They seem to be favorites of illustrators and the designers of children's literature.

The literary education of children is not complete unless they have more than sampled the folk literature that is available to them. From the Nursery Rhymes of very early childhood, to the fairy tales, the fables and the hero tales for the middle grades, and the legends, myths, and epics for the upper grade youngster, the folktale is a part of the children's literary heritage. His culture and the culture of his ancestors speak to him from the folktale. The art of language, in its oldest form, is available to children in these tales.

Some teachers are not content with just presenting these tales to children for enjoyment only. These teachers believe that children should know about the origins of the folktales, from what places they have come and how they have been modified and changed through translation and usage. Some teachers even point out the motif patterns in these tales and discuss the theories of how these tales came into being. Children are fascinated to know, for example, that *Cinderella* is found in some 345 variations that have appeared in all parts of Europe, India, Egypt, and even among the Indians of America. They are amused by Richard Chase's *The Jack Tales* but are most interested in knowing that these American mountain tales are really old tales from England that grew from *Jack and the Beanstalk* to their present form, so beautifully told by Mr. Chase.

The teacher has a rich source available to her in the folktale if she wishes to increase literary awareness, appreciation, and history. This learning should not come at the expense of enjoyment, however. Literature for children is meant to delight and entertain—not to be put in the context of a task.

The folktale is often full of moral teaching, didactic material, and temperance truths. Beware of the "hammering home" of these ethics and morals. Children will see the truths inherent in many of these tales and do not need additional moralizing by the teacher. Children's resistance to this kind of teaching is amazing! It is best to leave it alone when there is the desire to help children learn to love literature.

The folktale is an important genre in children's literature. Our literary heritage is in these tales. We owe our children the riches that come from them.

## Summary

CHILDREN'S LITERATURE is an art form. It is an art form that combines the art of language and illustration into that special phenomenon, the children's trade book.

The many fine books that are available to children in the realm of their literature offer opportunities to experience the finest language in our culture. This use of language as an art provides youngsters with a model for language. Both as silent reading material and material read orally, some of the most creative and beautiful experiences the child has with our language comes from the pages of children's literature.

The child, in his first experiences with literature, often develops a pattern for reading that will be with him for the rest of his life. His literary environment in the classroom, therefore, needs to be good so that he is able to develop a taste for that which has literary quality. Literary taste can be encouraged if his literary environment offers him the best in literature.

The aesthetic education the elementary student can enjoy from interacting with good children's literature extends into the appreciation for and understanding of the art of illustration. Few sources offer the youngster an opportunity to view the world of the illustrator better than does the children's trade book. The creative use of media and the multiple ways the graphic artist communicates his story to his audience give children a rare opportunity to see and understand the divergence and validity of the graphic artist.

The children's trade book presents opportunities for children to experience the use of language in many forms, other than prose. Poetry, the art of the playwright, the creativity of dramatic play all spring to life from the pages of good selections of literature for children. Likewise, the old magic of the folktale is available to children in many handsome volumes.

Children's trade books are an art form in themselves. The aesthetic experiences children can gain from these books make their use, for this one aspect alone, most valid.

# EXERCISES
## FOR THE TEACHER

1. Discuss with your classmates the value of oral reading to children. Make a bibliography of books that lend themselves to oral reading.

2. Compare the styles of several well-known children's illustrators. How will you help children note the similarities and differences in these styles?

3. "Read" a picture book without the text, then read the text. How close together are the stories?

4. Try a session with creative drama. . .

5. Prepare a lesson plan that will employ strategies that will help children understand the art of language in a good trade book.

6. Find a good collection of children's poetry. Prepare several for oral reading and present them to your class.

7. If possible, interview an elementary teacher and find out how often she reads orally to children.

8. Locate a collection of children's dramatic literature. Prepare a drama on a tape recorder, or live, for the class.

9. Recall your experiences with poetry in the elementary school. How will you modify these experiences for your pupils?

10. What picture books can you locate that are appropriate for children in the middle and upper grades?

11. Interview an artist, or a professor of art, and ask him about the importance of children's book illustrations in the art education of youngsters.

# SUGGESTED READINGS

APPLEGATE, MAUREE. *Easy in English*. New York: Harper and Row Publishers, 1964.

ARBUTHNOT, MAY HILL. *Children and Books*. 3rd ed. Chicago: Scott, Foresman and Company, 1964.

————, and ROOT, SHELDON, JR. *Time for Poetry*. Chicago: Scott, Foresman and Company, 1968.

ARNSTEIN, FLORA J. *Adventure Into Poetry*. Stanford, Calif.: Stanford University Press, 1951.

BLINN, MARJEANNE JENSEN, comp. *Summoned by Books*. New York: The Viking Press, Inc., 1965.

BURNS, PAUL C., and LOWE, ALBERTA. *The Language Arts in Childhood Education*. Chicago: Rand McNally & Company, 1966.

CHAMBERS, DEWEY. *Literature for Children: Storytelling and Creative Drama*. Dubuque, Iowa: Wm. C. Brown Company, 1970.

CIANCIOLO, PATRICIA. *Literature for Children: Illustrations in Children's Books*. Dubuque, Iowa: Wm. C. Brown Company, 1970.

DALLMAN, MARTHA. *Teaching the Language Arts in the Elementary School*. Dubuque, Iowa: Wm. C. Brown Company, 1966.

DAWSON, MILDRED A., and ZOLLINGER, MARIAN. *Guiding Language Learning*. New York: Harcourt, Brace & World, Inc., 1963.

DUFF, ANNIS. *Bequest of Wings*. New York: The Viking Press, Inc., 1954.

FITZGERALD, BURDETTE. *Let's Act the Story*. Palo Alto, Calif.: The Fearon Press, 1957.

HAVILAND, VIRGINIA. *Children's Literature: A Guide to Reference Sources*. Washington, D. C.: Library of Congress, 1966.

HOLLOWELL, LILLIAN. *A Book of Children's Literature*. 3rd ed. New York: Holt, Rinehart and Winston, Inc., 1966.

HUCK, CHARLOTTE S., and YOUNG KUHN, DORIS. *Children's Literature in the Elementary School.* 2nd ed. New York: Holt, Rinehart and Winston, Inc., 1968.

KLEMIN, DIANA. *The Art of Art for Children's Books.* New York: Clarkson N. Potter, Inc., 1966.

LAMB, POSE, ed. *Guiding Children's Language Learning.* Dubuque, Iowa: Wm. C. Brown Company, 1967.

LARRICK, NANCY. *Teacher's Guide to Children's Books.* Columbus, Ohio: Charles E. Merrill Books, Inc., 1960.

NATIONAL CONFERENCE ON RESEARCH IN ENGLISH. *Development of Taste in Literature.* Champaign, Ill.: National Council of Teachers of English, 1963.

SMITH, DORA V. *Fifty Years of Children's Books.* Champaign, Ill.: The National Council of Teachers of English.

SMITH, JAMES A. *Creative Teaching of Reading and Literature in the Elementary School.* Boston: Allyn and Bacon, 1967.

SMITH, JAMES S. *A Critical Approach to Children's Literature.* New York: McGraw-Hill Book Company, 1967.

SMITH, LILLIAN. *The Unreluctant Years.* New York: The Viking Press, Inc., 1953.

SECTION TWO

# How Books Can
# Affect Children

*Chapter V*

# THE DIDACTIC THEORY

*The history of literature* reveals that "The Book" has been considered through the ages to be a didactic instrument. Its purpose was to teach and instruct, to inculcate values, ethics, and morals and to pave the road to salvation on earth and beyond.

The Bible, of course, is the prime example of the power of the printed word on the lives of those who interact with it. Entire cultures, with their laws and mores, are based on the old Judaic-Christian teaching found in the testaments. That one book, The Bible, has probably affected world culture and history more than any one, single instrument. Its teachings comprise much of today's fabric of living in the western world.

To consider The Bible in the same light as one considers literature by its common definition, however, would certainly be faulty. The Bible is a repository of a religion and a philosophy. It is a source from which philosophical and religious teaching springs. It has been a wellspring for cultures. Literature, as it is usually defined, is not thought of in this manner. Writings of a sacred nature, such as The Bible, have no place in the consideration of a discussion about the effect of literature on the lives of readers in our context. As a result, The Bible and other sacred writings cannot be compared as a literary genre with the literature under consideration in this book.

It has been common belief, however, from early times that books (fiction) are a means of influencing the lives of their readers. There is evidence from five centuries of writings that men have not only held this assumption to be valid, but have, as a result of their beliefs, included varying amounts of didactic content in their books.

As far back as 1473, Scott De Bury's *Philobiblon* stated: "These (books) are masters who instruct us without rods or ferules, without hard words and anger, without clothes or money." The idea that books instructed men has been a thread in pedagogical writing. These writers have intimated that literature provides vicarious experiences that will allow the reader to explore his world and modify the values and attitudes he holds. "Reading maketh a full man" wrote Francis Bacon (1561–1626), indicating to his generation and to those that followed his beliefs concerning the effect of books upon the development of a person. Likewise, Thomas Carlyle (1795–1881) wrote, "Literary men are . . . a perpetual priesthood," thus telling us that, indeed, values and attitudes are affected by the books that one reads.

More contemporary literary professionals echo those of the past. Katherine Logan wrote, "The book you read may have much to do with your choosing of the road." Budd Schulberg writes of today's world and books, but still harks back to the quotations of Bacon and Carlyle, when he says, "In the flush of T.V. spectaculars, wider and wider screeneramas and all the rest of the frightful, fruitful mechanical advancements, the book is still the essential civilizing influence, able to penetrate the unknowns of human aspirations."[1]

The children's trade book certainly has been a good example of this didactic approach through the centuries. Those pieces of children's literature that remain with us in a relatively unedited

---

[1] E. Paul Hovey, comp., *The Treasury of Inspirational Anecdotes, Quotations and Illustrations* (Westwood, N. Y.: Fleming H. Revell Company, 1959), p. 52.

form, such as *Aesop's Fables* or the *Fables of La Fontaine*, attest to this content. Children were to be taught "the correct way" from these books. Morals, manners, and religion were prime purposes of these early offerings in children's literature. If enjoyment and delight occurred along the way, so much the better. Of course, too much enjoyment could be sinful!

In the United States, since colonial times, one of the most commonly agreed upon functions of education has been that, among other things, it is to transmit to the student the values, morals, and ethics held by the dominant members of the society. Literature, in one form or another, has always been a part of the school curriculum, and that literature has been of a didactic nature.

The first children's book to be published in the New World appeared in 1646. It was written by John Cotton and its full title was: *Milk for Babes, Drawn out of the Breasts of Both Testaments, Chiefly for the Spiritual Nourishment of Boston Babes in either England, but may be of like use for any children.* It was followed by editions of *The New England Primer*, published as early as 1691. Both books were as heavily loaded with moral, ethical, and value-influencing content as the titles suggest. The purpose of those early American children's books was, of course, to help assure the transmission of the Puritan ideals.

Reading for patriotism, good citizenship, and industry was the purpose of the well-known *Eclectic Readers* by William H. McGuffey. McGuffey's books were so widely used from 1834 to 1900 that one could almost say these readers comprised the elementary curriculum in literature. One obvious assumption upon which these books were based was the continuing one that literature can, indeed, be used as a vehicle for the transmission of cultural ideals.

Most authorities who are concerned about the history of children's literature agree that this purpose of children's books changed little up to the beginning of the twentieth century. With the new century, the emphasis seemed to be on good manners. Children were to be taught how to be ladies and gentlemen through their literature. The earlier purpose of scaring them out of their wits through their books gave way to a gentler, but not less didactic approach of correct, gentle living.

Students of literature for children do concede that in the present era, the didactic content seems to be less. This may be due to a more sophisticated, thorough understanding of how children develop and learn. The fields of psychology and education are sciences that no longer subscribe to the old approaches of inculcation and learning. At any rate, literature for children in the last half of our century appears to have lessened the old didactic austerity.

Does this apparent reduction in didactic content in children's books mean that we no longer believe that what children read will affect them? Has the theory that "books maketh the full man" been discarded in favor of another idea about the role children's books play in the development of youngsters? Hardly! This theory is still a widely accepted one. Children's books are carefully scrutinized and are still thought to be important instruments in the growth and development of children.

## HOW BOOKS AFFECT CHILDREN

With few exceptions, it is an almost universal belief among the experts of children's literature that children's trade books can influence the attitudes and behavior of young people. These experts argue that learning comes as a result of experiences. Interacting with literature is an experience and can thus affect the learning syndrome. The vicarious experiences that a youngster has with books can stir his curiosity and stimulate his mind. It can give him a model for living which can affect his attitude toward life. The young reader can, through interacting with his literature, increase his understanding of himself and other people and develop insights and wisdom that can stand him in good stead as he develops toward maturity.

The belief that children's literature affects his development can further, some say, affect his values. Montgomery Johnston's comments lead us to believe that children's books will help children develop values of good versus evil, love of animals, love for independence, and a great many other values including the important values of integration in a multi-cultured society.[2]

Reading of children's literature is likewise thought by some as a good chance for children to compare one set of values with another. The content of children's books will help children understand the shading between good and evil, right and wrong, black and white. Understanding this shading can help children understand better the conflicts and desires between men and societies. This opportunity to involve himself, at least vicariously, with the ideas, viewpoints, problems, and difficulties of others, helps the youngster understand cultures, both of the past and present.

Some authorities believe that interacting with children's books can be psychologically therapeutic. As children read selections they will very likely meet characters who have problems much like their own. How these characters solve their problems can be most beneficial to youngsters attempting a solution of their own problems.

Ruth Strickland sums up what most authorities believe about the relationship of literature and child development when she wrote: "Children love books because by nature they desire to know and experience. The stories in which they live help to form their philosophy of life and to enter into their common humanity."[3]

Today's American school is concerned about the value education of children. This concern has reflected itself in the curriculum of our schools. Curricular emphasis in this area has been called by several names. These include: (1) moral education, (2) character education, and (3) citizenship education. Each of these terms, in a broad sense, expresses that goal of education which is concerned with fostering the development of a worthy person.

Educators have discussed at length, both philosophically and pedagogically, the process by which value learning is acquired. In general, most agree that good literature can exert a positive in-

---

[2] Montgomery Johnston, "The Classics of Children's Literature," *Elementary English* XXXIX, No. 5 (May, 1962), p. 412.

[3] Ruth Strickland, "What Thou Lovest Well Remains," *Elementary English* XXXVIII, No. 2 (February, 1961), p. 63–73.

fluence on young readers by fostering the development of a set of worthy values.

It is interesting to note that while authorities agree and have agreed for years about the positive effect literature can exert on the development of a youngster, there is remarkably little research to back up these opinions. It has only been in recent years that any attempt has been made to determine scientifically whether or not literature does influence the child's developing social conscience. Even research is not clear on the extent of this influence.

The research that has been done seems to cluster into two general areas: (1) the effect of books on children and (2) book content, or what is in these books that can affect children.

## RESEARCH ON THE EFFECTS
## OF BOOKS ON CHILDREN

Research in this area has been recent and is inconclusive. Most studies do agree that literature *may* be an important instrument in the child's value development. But, if such learning does take place, the extent of that learning and its permanence has yet to be determined. Much of the research available is unfortunately ambiguous and is laden with conjecture and opinion. It is difficult to determine the effect of children's reading on their value growth from research carried on during the past few years. Some work has been done, however, and it is worthy of attention.

Some early studies showed that a positive relationship does exist under a controlled environment. The group of studies conducted by Douglas Waples, *et al.* in 1940, dealing with literature and attitude change do attest to the idea that change can be effected through selected reading materials.[4] This study used college students as subjects. The experimenters inventoried the students' attitudes before and after submitting them to certain reading

---

[4] Douglas Waples, Bernard Berelson, and Franklyn Bradshaw, *What Reading Does to People: A Summary of Evidence on the Social Effects of Reading and a Statement of Problems for Research* (Chicago: University of Chicago Press, 1940), p. 8.

materials. The reading material was specifically designed to test attitudes toward religious beliefs, racial bias, and economic status. Waples reports that these studies repeatedly showed that reading can influence and even change values and attitudes.

The Waples report does admit that the results are in generalized terms and that its validity is limited by the concentration upon one social group, college students. The report also admits that the brevity of the reading material and the pointed nature of the experiment may have had an effect on the results.

Despite these limitations, the Waples studies are significant. They do show that under certain conditions reading can affect attitude. How long this change will last, or how deeply imbedded the change will be, is, of course, another question.

The brilliant work of the late David H. Russell has given us some of our most insightful comments concerning children and personality development in relation to literature. Dr. Russell believed that books for children are one of the main sources at work in helping a child develop a personality. He was quick to admit, however, that research on this assumption was missing. He wrote: "This evidence from the studies of reading interests and investigations in other forms of children's literature is notably inconclusive about the role of identification in children's literature experiences."[5]

Russell indicated at the time (1949) that some studies gave a few suggestions of possible identifications in children's literature, but, unfortunately, too many of those studies were concerned with the mere listing of favorite books or types of books without any deeper research into why children like what they do, or how reading of that material affects them. The concern is also true today.

Russell in 1958 again stated his concern for the lack of research in this area. He admitted the difficulty a researcher would have in determining exactly what influence reading has on the personality development of the child. Just how one could isolate the effect books have on personality development from all the other influencing agents was admittedly a task that offered a real challenge.

---

[5] David H. Russell, "Identification Through Literature," *Childhood Education* XXV (May, 1949), p. 397.

After reviewing some seventy-three studies on the impact of reading he concluded: "We are beginning to get clues about the kinds of reactions we can expect from individuals of different backgrounds, interest, and personality, but it is difficult to disentangle the influences of reading from those of other activities."[6]

Russell's conclusion is echoed by Henry Meckle. Meckle indicates that researchers attempting to measure the effects of reading on subjects have not been successful because not enough depth psychological evidence pertaining to the subjects has been collected before the research on reading and its effect begins. He remarks:

> The study of responses to literature is complicated by the fact that what may appear to be purely literary responses or intellectual judgements may in terms of subconscious motivations, be actually quite another kind of response. Thus an adequate description of responses to literature requires analysis not only in terms of literary components or surface motivations, but also in terms of the insights of clinical psychologists into human personality. This requirement holds especially true for the dynamic mechanisms involved in identification made by readers with characters in fiction, in reactions to emotional situations, and in response to content involving emotionally charged attitudes such as social sensitivity or prejudice. Consequently, research on responses to literature should be designed to use case studies of subjects about whose personality organization and emotional pattern much is known. Such research remains to be done.[7]

Hilda Taba's research with the Intergroup Education Project[8] designed to develop social sensitivity is a major contribution in

---

[6] David H. Russell, "Some Research on the Impact of Reading," *English Journal* XXXXVII (September, 1958), p. 398.

[7] Henry C. Meckel, "Research on Teaching Composition and Literature," *Handbook of Research on Teaching*, ed. N. L. Gage (Chicago: Rand McNally & Company, 1963), p. 966.

[8] Hilda Taba, *With Perspectives on Human Relations: A Study of Peer Group Dynamics in an Eighth Grade* (Washington, D. C.: American Council on Education, 1955).

helping us understand more about value modification and learning as a result of interaction with literature for children. Taba's work with a group of eighth graders in helping them overcome their ethnocentric orientation to values and become sensitive to other cultural groups and their value orientation is most significant. She offers techniques of actually working with books and children in a way designed to modify attitude.

Taba wrote:

The development of a cosmopolitan sensitivity and a capacity to respond to human problems, values, and feelings is a central task in education for human relations. Each individual grows up in a somewhat limiting cultural shell by virtue of the fact that the intermediate primary groups in which a growing person is socialized are culturally unique.... The experiences in the hemmed-in cultural climates tend to cultivate ethnocentricity, or a tendency to interpret all other persons' behavior, values, and motivations in terms of one's own values.[9]

Taba indicated that there is a continuing social distance from the primary family groups because of the increasing mobility of the culture. Core values, she wrote, are therefore becoming more and more inaccessible. One result, Taba believed, is ethnocentricity. This is a major cause of prejudice, she reported. Taba further indicated that major ways are needed to eliminate ethnocentricity in judgment and conduct and to come to a more realistic look at the realities of life.

She continued:

The problem of maintaining a core of democratic values is serious in a society with a multiplicity of cultural pockets maintained by social segregation. There is an urgent need to explore the means for extension of sensitivity, for developing a capacity of understanding across barriers and the ability to bridge cultural and psychological distances.
One way to meet these problems is for the schools to introduce learning experiences which help build a transition from both

---

[9] *Ibid.*, p. 100.

the egocentric orientation to people and life peculiar to child-hood and the ethnocentric orientation peculiar to social learn-ing, to a new orientation which includes a capacity to identify not only with known persons but also with the values of un-known groups and the generalized values of humanity.
One method used by the project on Intergroup Education was to use literature to help extend social sensitivity and the ca-pacity to identify with other people.[10]

Reading programs for the project were planned on the follow-ing hypotheses: (1) that fiction is one potent source for internaliz-ing values different from the current experience of a given group; (2) that by inducing identification with characters, problems, and feelings expressed in fiction individuals can be helped to make a transition from ethnocentric orientation to an "other-centered" orientation; and (3) that an open-ended discussion of stories is one way to accomplish this end.

The Taba experimental curriculum attempted to extend social sensitivity. A basic sequential program was organized on the basis of a careful diagnosis of the eighth graders' own problems and concerns as discovered from their diaries and other writings with particular attention to limitations in the area of social understand-ing. Books were chosen carefully to reflect the same or similar problems as found in the diagnosis but describing different or con-trasting contexts and experiences. There were systematic oppor-tunities, through discussion, to analyze the behavior, problems, and motivations of the characters in these books or stories and to com-pare them with the student's own experiences. There was also continuous emphasis upon understanding the feelings in human situations as matters to be considered when interpreting the mean-ing of these situations, in judging the validity of the problems, or the solution encountered in reacting. A continuing effort was made to apply and transfer whatever was learned in one context to other and different contexts.

At the end of the one-year study, Taba had these conclusions concerning the use of literature as an aid in expanding the chil-dren's value orientations:

---

[10] *Ibid.*, p. 101.

1.   That the method of reading and discussing fiction organized around life problems of students is effective in extending sensitivity to human values and in objectifying orientation to human relations.

2.   It is evident that a wide range of personality types and intellectual ability can be accommodated and affected by this method.

3.   It is evident that the use of fiction for teaching understanding of human values is a method which allows a comfortable integration of emotional insights and of concept building, and that this integration is of aid in deepening understanding and developing ability to transfer.

4.   The method also seems of great promise in developing understanding of fairly complicated concepts and rendering them applicable to entirely new areas of life.

5.   It was clear that the analysis of values and feelings and of their meaning in many personalized situations affected (positively) the content of the peer group life.[11]

Several other studies followed. The one by W. Loban and what appears to be a follow up of this work by Margaret Heaton and Helen Lewis, later revised by Muriel Crosby (the new edition by Virginia Reid is due in the 1970s) are pertinent to the concepts under this discussion.

Loban's study found that mere exposure to stories read aloud to adolescents did not bring about any apparent change in attitudes held by members of the group tested. He found that discussion techniques were necessary if the students were to achieve any of the desired insights of social sensitivity that the study intended.[12]

Crosby's *Reading Ladders for Human Relations* follows through by offering techniques about how books can help foster the growth of sensitivity. She suggests that a reading program must be so organized as to provide these experiences for the reader:[13]

---

[11] *Ibid.*, p. 137.

[12] W. Loban, *Literature and Social Sensitivity* (Champaign, Ill.: National Council of Teachers of English, 1954).

[13] Muriel Crosby, ed., *Reading Ladders for Human Relations*, 4th ed. (Washington, D. C.: American Council on Education, 1964).

1. The reader must have the opportunity to identify himself with the characters in this book through vicarious emotional experiences.

2. The reader must be encouraged to recognize how the emotional experiences in the book provide an extension of his own experiences.

3. The reader must be encouraged to identify different kinds of human relationships, recognizing in them blocks or aids to communication and to the growth of common purpose. He must live in a social environment where these aspects of human relationships are commented upon, highlighted, and analyzed objectively. A classroom discussion may provide this social environment.[14]

This technique and its success as reported by Taba and Loban, and urged in the approach suggested by Crosby, is approved by other experts in the field. Meckel restates the validity of the discussion method when he writes:

Since pupils left to their own resources are likely not to acquire the insights desired by the teacher, the discussion method becomes of great significance in the effective teaching of literature. Through discussion, the teacher can lead pupils to perceptions and discoveries that they are not likely to apprehend or understand without his guidance.[15]

Most authorities in the field are quick to indicate, however, that a book, or any other single device, for that matter, cannot hope to remake a child's character or personality. But, they feel, if a book is properly handled as a teaching device, it has a strong potential as a molder of a child's view of himself and his world.

David Russell's point of view seems to summarize the opinions and research concerning the effect books have on children. He indicated that reading is responding. The response, he wrote, may be solely at the surface level of "calling" the word. The reading act may be at a somewhat deeper level of understanding the ex-

---

[14] *Ibid.*, p. 22.

[15] Meckel, *loc. cit.*, p. 997.

plicit meaning of the sentence, paragraph or passage. Or, it can be at a third level. It may involve going beyond the facts to new and personal meanings.[16]

Dr. Russell indicated that the young reader can be helped to see that some poems and stories have hidden meanings that must be explored and, if possible, understood. Although the child will not name them directly, these meanings and symbols may represent some of the important, unifying ideas of our culture, such as the importance of the individual or the value of cooperative effort. Russell indicated that these concepts will probably not be stated explicitly in the story. Therefore, they must be "read into" the story by the reader. Usually, the young reader needs help in finding such symbols and deeper meaning.

Russell wrote:

> In literature children and adolescents can find many of man's most important social-ethical ideas. Our values are the things we live by...values are usually described in the lovely words of our language, such as truth, justice, loyalty and faith. These are puzzling and difficult ideas for adults and even more for children, and yet they are the foundation of society. A child's or adolescent's grasp of such concepts is slow agrowing. Only a wide variety of experiences can give some understanding to tolerance or perseverance or sacrifice, but sometimes the process of getting to understand such ideas can be quickened through literature.[17]

While we admittedly do not know the extent the effect literature may have on the developing personality of children or how long any such effect will last, most authorities in the field believe a positive relationship exists. The studies done do give us clues to this phenomenon but do not give us the empirical research needed to make a definite statement concerning it. It is foolish to discard the adage that "books maketh the full man" because of the current lack of scientific proof. Because we are currently unable to measure a truth does not mean it lacks substance.

---

[16] David H. Russell, "Personal Values in Reading," *The Reading Teacher* XII (January, 1958), pp. 3–9.

[17] *Ibid.*, p. 7.

Certainly, the concern to help children interpret what they read in their literature is a valid one. A book, by itself, in the hands of a child is not as potent an instrument for learning as is a book aided by a teacher who knows the art of teaching. There is nothing magical or mystical about children's literature. Bringing books and children together does not automatically assure learning. Learning must be planned for and worked toward. Children's literature is a potent source for helping children learn about the world and their place in it. Literature, however, must be augmented by the fine art of teaching.

## RESEARCH ON THE CONTENT
## OF CHILDREN'S LITERATURE

If, indeed, children's books do affect the attitudinal growth of youngsters and a positive correlation does exist between children's literature and personality development, what is in children's literature that can affect the child? If these books for children are didactic instruments, what do they contain that can be used to help children develop values, attitudes, beliefs, and the like?

Content analysis of children's literature is a recent development in educational research. The results of this research are not conclusive because too few studies have been completed. What has been done is perhaps trend setting but one cannot build a valid conclusion concerning the content of children's literature in relation to the didactic theory based upon the results of a few studies. The research that has been completed, however, is significant in that it does give us some insight into the content of children's books as set forth within the limitations of the research designed. It would be a dangerous assumption to make a universal statement concerning the content of American children's literature based upon the little evidence that we have from research.

An early study dealing with the content analysis of children's literature was done by John Shepard.[18] Shepard reported a study that dealt with the treatment of characters in popular children's

---

[18] John P. Shepard, "The Treatment of Characters in Popular Children's Fiction," *Elementary English* XXXIX (November, 1962), p. 675.

fiction. He read sixteen children's books that were reported by parents, teachers, and librarians to be the books most often selected by children in the middle and upper grades. These books spanned, according to Shepard, nearly a century of writing.

The study was designed to compare, in six categories, the favorable and unfavorable character in these books: (*1*) race, (*2*) nationality, (*3*) religion, (*4*) physical appearance, (*5*) socio-economic status, and (*6*) standards of conduct and attitude.

He found the characters in these books to be as follows: The heroes and heroines were clean, white, healthy, handsome, Protestant, middle class people. The villains were portrayed most often as ugly, physically undesirable, non-Caucasians, either very wealthy or of the poorer classes.

The favorable characters in the books analyzed outnumbered the unfavorable almost three to one (152-60). The Americans portrayed in these books were almost always the heroes. Few American villains were found. The non-Caucasians (most often non-Americans) were generally portrayed in a very negative way. They were unattractive physically and acted in an unintelligent, cruel, or reprehensible way.

Religious affiliations of the characters in these books were rarely indicated. The Protestant beliefs, however, were in the majority for the heroes.

The Shepard study, as reported, does not give evidence of how the characteristics identified were chosen nor how the results were tabulated. The books chosen for analysis were based upon the opinions of parents, teachers, and librarians. The number of subjects contacted was not revealed and no attempt to validate the popularity of the books was made.

Shepard's concluding remarks ask to what extent children really respond to the characters found in his analysis of children's books. He confesses little is known about the effect, when he writes:

> The literature on the effects of reading is full of assumptions, and nearly empty of definitive, conclusive findings. It seems necessary to follow our common sense feelings that stories do affect children until and if the reverse is ever proven.[19]

---

[19] *Ibid.*, p. 672.

David C. McClelland reports that during a research project in social psychology he had an opportunity to read and analyze children's trade books from forty different countries.[20] He analyzed these books to locate values in them and compare them to the values held by the adult population of the countries. McClelland concludes that popular children's literature reflects the values of the people in the countries where the children's books were analyzed.

He found themes stressed in these books that reflected what he thought were the underlying values of the people. In the Middle Eastern countries of Turkey, Lebanon, and Tunisia, for example, he found the theme of cleverness stressed in most books for children. In Chile and Japan, he found the emphasis on kindness and obligation common. The German books stressed loyalty, while American books for children stressed cooperation. McClelland indicates that while most themes are present in all the books analyzed, certain ones are stressed, giving evidence, he feels, to the theory that children's literature does reflect the value orientation of a nation. He writes:

> The conclusion is inescapable that popular stories for children reflect what the people in the country value most, what they think is important. And children learn from reading stories that adults regard as important.[21]

McClelland takes a firm stand on the effect these books have in molding the child's personality and value structure when he writes:

> I believe that children acquire the values or ethical ideas expressed in the stories, even without conscious and deliberate attempts to abstract them. It is the abstraction process that is difficult, not the ideas themselves. I believe that Middle Eastern

---

[20] David C. McClelland, "Values in Popular Literature for Children," *Childhood Education*, No. 3 (November, 1963), p. 135. Reprinted by permission of David C. McClelland and the Association for Childhood Education International, 3615 Wisconsin Avenue, N. W., Washington, D. C. Copyright November, 1963 by the Association.

[21] *Ibid.*, p. 136.

children learn naturally and easily from what they read that cleverness is a good thing, just as American children learn that working together is usually the best way of doing things. Children come to take such ideas for granted because that's the way things 'are' or 'happen' in the stories they read.[22]

Alma Cross Homze reports findings dealing with the content of children's fiction in an area of interpersonal relations.[23] Her study attempted to find discernible changes in interpersonal relations described in children's fiction books between 1920 and 1960. The content analysis method was used with samples of children's books chosen at five-year intervals from 1920 to 1960.

Three major areas of interpersonal relations were studied by Homze. They were: (1) adult-child relationships, behavior instigated by an adult and received by a child, (2) child-adult relationships, behavior expressed by a child and directed at an adult, and (3) child-child relationships, behavior initiated by a child and expressed to another child.

Homze's conclusions concerning the interpersonal relations in children's fiction do indicate a change in the trend since 1920. Some of her findings are:

1. That behaviors described in children's books indicate a trend toward fewer expressions of affection among child and adult characters.
2. That children's books reflect the increasing middle class population.
3. That a trend exists that takes the characters from a rural location to urban situations for interaction.
4. That children's books describe a predominately homogeneous population of American Caucasians.
5. That there is an increasing number of male child characters.[24]

---

[22] Ibid.

[23] Alma Cross Homze, "Interpersonal Relationships in Children's Literature 1920–1960" (Unpublished Ed. D. dissertation, Department of Elementary Education, Pennsylvania State University, 1963).

[24] Ibid., p. 132.

The study further concludes that the data collected can be interpreted to mean:

1. That child characters are increasingly outspoken in their relationships with adults.
2. That child characters are becoming more critical of adult characters.
3. That child characters increasingly assert their independence in relationships with other children.
4. That there is increasing competition among adult and child characters.
5. That adult characters are decreasingly critical of, and less authoritarian in, their relationships with children.
6. That child characters increasingly prefer to interact in unsupervised areas.
7. That children's books describe fewer farm and more middle class occupations.[25]

Homze makes no effort to indicate how these interpersonal relations found in the books affect the child. Her study was designed simply to report changes in interpersonal relations as portrayed in children's fiction books from 1920 to 1960.

The Dewey Chambers study of 1965 was concerned with social value influencing material in children's literature. The study contained evidence from books published during one year by two firms: (1) Viking Press and (2) Harcourt, Brace and World. The data were concerned with value influencing material which was judged present in fiction books for children ages five through nine years. The author measured the nature and degree of intensity of such social value influencing material which he found in the books analyzed.[26]

After developing an instrument to determine the extent to which these values were present in the selected books, he gathered

---

[25] *Ibid.*, p. 135.

[26] Dewey Woods Chambers, "An Exploratory Study of Social Values in Children's Literature" (Unpublished Ed. D. dissertation, College of Education, Wayne State University, Detroit, Mich., 1965).

data which revealed the frequency of appearance of the social values as well as the intensity of their treatment. The devised instrument was also used to determine the predominant vehicle, or symbolic medium, through which these values were expressed.

Seven social values were explored in this study. They were those values which dealt with:

1.  Aspects of the person himself as an individual.
2.  Selected social values—fairness, honesty, kindness, cooperation, and commitment.
3.  Aspects of peer group relations.
4.  Aspects of family living.
5.  Aspects of neighborhood and community living.
6.  Aspects of world and national living.
7.  Aspects of time passage and social change.

The study reported a number of conclusions drawn from the gathered data. Some conclusions reached were:

1.  In general, the books analyzed gave minimum opportunity to explore the social values defined in the study.
2.  It was suggested that this limited treatment of the social values in these books was due to several causes: (a) fear of loss of sales, (b) fear of losing acceptance by writers and publishers, (c) lack of understanding of the importance of dealing with such matters in children's books, and (d) the opinion of editors and writers that children of this age have little ability to deal with such concepts.
3.  The social values identified in the study, as judged important by cited experts, were found to be presented in a uniformly weak manner.
4.  The two publishing houses compared in the study seemed to be affected by similar forces in shaping their editorial policies so that little difference could be found between their respective treatment of social values in their publications for children five through nine.
5.  The vehicle of representation of the social value was predominately in terms of human beings. Hence, most current

fiction written for children of the prescribed age is of the realistic variety.[27]

This study did not attempt to determine to what extent these books and their content affected children. It was a content analysis to gain insight into what is in children's literature that can affect the youngster, if indeed, it affects him at all.

The Heath Lowry study of 1966 offers further evidence about what didactic material is contained in children's books. His study was concerned with the presence of that content in the Newbery Medal Award winning books from 1922 through 1965 which may influence children's learning of American middle class moral and ethical values. The study used the process of content analysis to gather data for answering four questions: (1) Are American middle class moral and ethical values present in this chosen list of books? (2) If such value content is present, to what degree of frequency and intensity has it been found? (3) What variations, if any, can be measured in the presence, frequency, and intensity of these values as they have been treated in five-year spans during the forty-five year period? (4) Is there evidence of trending in the data collected from the period studies?[28]

Lowry's work isolated fifteen values thought to be important in American society. They were:

> Responsibility of Church (Religion)
> Civic and Community Responsibility
> Freedom and Liberty
> Initiative and Achievement
> Justice and Equality
> Self-Reliance
> Loyalty
> Responsibility to Family
> Importance of Education

---

[27] *Ibid.*, pp. 81–82.

[28] Heath Ward Lowry, "An Exploratory Study of American Middle-Class Moral and Ethical Values Found in the John Newbery Medal Books" (Unpublished Ed. D. dissertation, University of the Pacific, Stockton, Calif., 1966).

Sexual Morality
Cleanliness and Neatness
Good Manners
Honesty in All things
Sanctity of Marriage
Thrift and Hard work.

The conclusions that Lowry reached at the end of his content analysis of the Newbery Award Winners were precise and exact. Some of the general conclusions from his study were:

1. Some of the identified criteria of values were present in all of the books analyzed; likewise all of the values sought were present in some of the books.

2. The moral and ethical values used in the study were generally found to be treated by the authors in a positive manner. However, the judged intensity of treatment was only in moderate measure throughout the books.

3. If one assumes that the Newbery Medal Winners are charged with didactic material in a traditional manner, this assumption can be challenged.

4. Frequently, the books having the strongest intensity of value treatment were set in early America during Colonial times, or at least during the eras of westward movement by pioneering settlers.

5. Some of the books which did not show an overall emphasis on the criteria of values frequently gave a strong degree of intensity to several of the basic values.

6. An interesting relationship exists between current social problems, e.g., race relations, high divorce rate, sexual promiscuity, prevalent examples of dishonesty and the lack of strong values dealing with these problems in the books analyzed in the study.

7. Current curricular practices which promote "human relations" (value orientation), through books such as these, can be seriously challenged.

8. The Committee which chooses the Newbery Medal

books does so solely on the basis of literary merit rather than didactic content.[29]

The Lowry study offers dramatic evidence concerning value influencing didactic material in some of our finest American children's literature. If we are able to transfer the Lowry conclusions to the wide range of literature for children, many of our traditional thoughts about the effects of books on children may not be as valid as we might like to believe.

Research concerning the effect books have on children's personality development, as well as the research designed to analyze the findings, is admittedly sparse. Educators and psychologists have long been operating on an educated opinion and have proceeded professionally on that opinion. Empirical evidence to give support or to negate these opinions is lacking. Content analysis, at least in two cases, gives us cause to wonder if there is sufficient content in these children's books to affect positive personality growth.

The evidence we do have does make one point quite clear: additional scholarly research in this area is badly needed. We need to know more about what effect books have on children and how long any effect will last. We need also to know more about what is in children's fiction that can affect their personality development. We need to submit the age-old assumption that "books maketh the full man" to serious investigation to determine more about its truth and how we can utilize its great potential.

## BIBLIOTHERAPY

Bibliotherapy describes a technique designed to help children solve, or at least better understand, their problems by interacting with literature. It is founded on the theory that there is a relationship between vicarious experience and personality development. Bibliotherapy proposes that a youngster can identify with char-

---

[29] *Ibid.*, p. 127.

acters and situations in a book that are similar to his own problems. As he interacts with the book, he sees how the characters solve their problems and handle their difficulties. In doing so, he can perhaps find similar ways to solve his own problems. It is in this way that "therapy" happens.

In using this technique, a child is studied most carefully so that his problems and needs are understood. He is then introduced to a book that has a problem affecting the character that is similar to one that affects him. In his interaction with this book, the child sees how a problem like his is solved. With assistance from the teacher or psychologist, he discusses, evaluates, and attempts to transfer the solution in the book to his own problem.

As we have seen earlier in this chapter, the only really new aspect of this practice is its name. Literary men and educators have long advocated that interaction with literature will affect the values, attitudes, and behaviors of people. Hitler believed this so strongly, for example, that he burned books that were thought to be dangerous to the Nazi philosophy. Bibliotherapy or "therapy through books" is a somewhat modern term, refined by technique. It is by no means a new idea.

Likewise, this theory of bibliotherapy is supported by numerous and most valuable opinions but little actual research. Bibliotherapy, like any of the ideas about how books affect readers, shows tremendous possibility. As yet nothing has been measured or scientifically investigated so that we, as teachers, can use it with some degree of confidence. It seems to be most successful in some cases as reported by professionals but the reports are not based upon empirical research evidence. Professional literature has many testimonials that sing its praises and offer case studies where children seem to respond to therapy through books. While these case studies are most interesting and in some instances dramatic, no evidence is offered that a change in behavior results from interacting with just the books alone. Many other forces, such as attention to the problem of the child by a helping adult, may be equally important in helping the youngster arrive at a solution or an approach to solving his problem. We cannot blithely attribute all that some would like to attribute to bibliotherapy, without more research. To negate this technique, however, because the research we need does not exist would be foolish. It is a technique that shows great promise. It is a theory that is as old as the printed word. It is an assumption, however, that lacks scientific validity.

Some of the most impressive case studies that have been in professional literature recently have resulted in an interesting term: "Preventative Bibliotherapy." The implication in the term is that a problem does not need to exist currently to employ this technique but the technique is employed to help meet a problem that may loom in the near future. Preventative Bibliotherapy helps children understand a problem before that problem becomes a block in the child's development.

Examples of this kind of bibliotherapy might be illustrated by posing hypothetical problem situations and suggesting books that can be presented to children to help them see a problem with greater understanding.

1. *The integration of an all white school by Negro children.* Before this happens, the teacher might read to the resident children Marguerite de Angeli's *Bright April* or Natalie S. Carlson's *The Empty Schoolhouse*, among others. Through discussion of the characters and situations in the book, the classroom to be racially mixed may have an easier time adjusting.

2. *The presence of a retarded child.* The child may, in time, be the butt of jokes and cruel remarks. The reading and discussion of Taro Yashima's *Crow Boy*, or others like it, may stem the problem before it matures into a negative experience for all involved.

3. *The presence, or imminent presence, of a physically defective or handicapped child in the classroom.* By reading a book such as de Angeli's *Door in the Wall*, sufficient understanding can result so that mutual adjustment between the class and the physically handicapped child will be facilitated.

This type of activity has all kinds of possibilities for classroom teachers, as can easily be seen. Just what effect it will have on the youngsters who interact with the literature is not known. It can, however, have a very positive effect. Those that have employed this technique are most vocal in their appreciation of it. The writer's emotional response to this practice is very positive.

The process of bibliotherapy has variables. It is much more than simply understanding a child's problem or one that is about to occur by presenting a youngster with a book that will fix everything. Quite the contrary. The book that one offers to children for identification and vicarious problem solving is but one part of bibliotherapy.

Varying authors approach this process with different techniques. Most, however, will recommend that the following elements be present in any bibliotherapeutic attempt:

1. Bibliotherapy is not a passive process. It is an active one. The teacher or psychologist works intensively with the youngster to help him solve his problems. This active process is outlined in several sources. The best and most useful one for teachers, however, is Muriel Crosby's *Reading Ladders for Human Relations*. This fine source should be examined closely before any bibliotherapy is attempted.

2. In successful bibliotherapy the teacher or psychologist who applies it needs to know the content of children's books. This implies knowing more than the plot level of a book as gained from any number of the bibliographies available. What do these books contain that will be of value to the youngster? What is in them that can serve as a genesis for discussion? What do they contain that will add insight into the problem the child has? A good knowledge of children's literature is imperative for any professional who will use bibliotherapy.

3. The teacher who uses bibliotherapy must know counseling techniques. How does one help the child relate his problems to the problems found in the book? How does one go about helping the child transfer solutions from the book to himself?

4. It is important to realize that bibliotherapy can be a difficult, dangerous task. Any teacher who employs it should do so under the guidance of a trained psychologist. The purposes and goals of bibliotherapy should be clear in the mind

of the teacher. Bibliotherapy is not a general kind of exercise in well-being.

5. One who works with bibliotherapy needs to remember that children's responses to books will be highly individual. All books do not affect children in the same way. These books are not pills that guarantee the same results for all subjects.

6. We need to remember that we do not know as much as we should know about what reading does to students. We know how to teach reading but what happens to students with what they read is not thoroughly understood.

7. Anyone who works with bibliotherapy should keep abreast of the latest research and scholarly opinion in the field. Breakthroughs in this area are imminent.

Bibliotherapy is another way that literature can affect the lives of children. The entire didactic theory of literature in the lives of children, for that matter, offers exciting, creative, and fruitful opportunities for the teacher who will expand the world of children through books.

For the graduate student of professional education, few fields offer such vast research possibilities as the investigation of how literature affects children. The possibilities for individual and group research activities are seemingly endless.

We are currently operating under more assumptions than proven fact in this area. We, frankly, do not know how much effect books do have on the children that read them. We assume the effect is an important variable in the development of a child's personality and his view of life. We should continue to assume this until we have proof that this assumption is not true.

# EXERCISES
## FOR THE TEACHER

1. Make a list of books that had a deep effect on you as a child. Read them now. What elements in these books affected you? Will they likely affect other children in the same way?

2. Using the bibliography that follows these questions, find one study, article, or book that you would like to probe. Do so and report your findings to the class.

3. Find several examples of early children's literature (1700–1800s) and read them. Note the didactic content. Is content of the same nature present in today's children's books? Would it be acceptable?

4. Analyze the content of several books from one author. Is there a message that is consistent in his works?

5. Interview a school psychologist. Question him on the technique and value of bibliotherapy.

6. Discuss, with children, the meanings they derive from books. How can this discussion be turned into a valuable experience of learning and accepting other people's values?

7. Watch for articles and new research in the professional journals dealing with the effect of books on children.

# SUGGESTED READINGS

Brooks, Alice. *Developmental Values in Books.* Chicago: American Library Association, 1949.

Comer, Dorothea. "Using Literature to Extend Children's Experience," *Elementary English* (January, 1959), pp. 28–29.

Darling, Robert L. *Mental Hygiene and Books.* Hamden, Conn.: Shoe String Press, 1962.

Fenner, Phyllis. *The Proof of the Pudding: What Children Read.* New York: The John Day Company, Inc., 1957.

Gage, N. L., ed. *Handbook of Research on Teaching: A Project of the American Educational Research Association.* Chicago: Rand McNally & Company, 1963.

Hazard, Paul. *Books, Children and Men.* Translated by Marguerite Mitchell. Boston: The Horn Book, 1947.

Loban, W. *Literature and Social Sensitivity.* Champaign, Ill.: National Council of Teachers of English, 1954.

————. *Techniques of Promoting Understanding of People Through Reading.* Chicago: University of Chicago Press, 1947.

Porterfield, Austin. *Mirror Mirror.* Fort Worth, Tex.: Leo Potishman Foundation, 1957.

Russell, David H., and Shrodes, Caroline. "Contributions of Research in Bibliotherapy to the Language Arts Program," *The School Review*, LVIII (September, 1950), p. 335.

Wertham, Frederic. *Seduction of the Innocent.* New York: Holt, Rinehart and Winston, Inc., 1953.

Yutang, Lin. *The Importance of Understanding.* Cleveland, Ohio: World Publishing Company, 1963.

## Chapter VI

# CHILDREN'S LITERATURE AND CREATIVE THINKING

*A great deal of attention* has been focused recently upon the creative child. Teachers are concerned about how this child learns, how to foster his creative ability, and how to work the needs of these youngsters into the classroom program. Scholarly attention by both educators and psychologists has likewise been directed toward this creative quality in children.

The creative person is, after all, that person who will most likely build our new cities, find medical cures, feed our souls, and take us to Mars. He is the one who brings about change. He is also the one who will help us learn to live with change. In our modern society, and in the society to come, his value is difficult to estimate. Our concern for him, as educators, is timely.

Those who are erudite in the field of creativity and creative behavior tell us that *all* children are creative. To be sure, some are more creative than others, but creative potential is present in all people. The creative potential in the child can be compared, in certain ways, to the intelligence of youngsters. All children have intelligence. Some have a greater amount of intelligence than others. So it is with creativity. Intelligence, or that quality that is measured by the I.Q. test, can also be raised by providing certain environmental factors. So, the experts tell us, can the level of creativity be raised. Creativity, that special quality unique to our species, can be fostered, nurtured, enhanced, and improved. The curriculum in the modern schools reflects this truth. Classroom conditions can be set to develop the creative potential of our students.

Creativity has been defined many ways. Some say that creativity is an esoteric quality that belongs to a select few. Many confuse it with talent or giftedness. Creativity to a working educator means something quite different. James A. Smith defines it in terms that are both eclectic and pragmatic. He defines it in the following way: "Creativity is sinking down taps into our past experiences and putting these selected experiences together into new patterns, new ideas or new products."[1] Many will disagree with this definition of creativity as over-simplified. For the purposes of this book this definition will suffice.

One of the major variables in helping children develop their creative potential is to provide opportunities for divergent thinking. With divergent thinking, facts, concepts, generalizations, and the like, are put to new uses. This kind of thinking encourages a number of solutions to a problem, not just one. Divergent thinking encourages many answers and ideas, not just one correct response. It allows an answer to a problem or a solution to open the gates to other problems or possibilities that spring from a solution or answer. The open-ended question and discussion exemplify the divergent thinking process in action.

Children's literature provides many opportunities for divergent and creative thinking. A classroom with a good literary environment probably can provide a better genesis for creative, divergent thinking than any other part of an elementary curriculum. \

---

[1] James A. Smith, *Setting Conditions for Creative Teaching in the Elementary School* (Boston: Allyn and Bacon, Inc., 1966), p. 4.

## CHILDREN'S LITERATURE AND THE
## STIMULATION OF DIVERGENT THINKING

When children read literature, they are involved in a highly creative act. They are, after all, reacting to nothing more than just the remains of ink on metal, arranged in an orderly fashion on paper. That they are able to bring life, emotion, adventure, beauty, images, and deep thought from those spots of ink is a wonder of the creative quality they possess. The interpretation of the printed language that man is able to manage is one of the most remarkable feats that our species has accomplished. When children begin to master this ability, the wonders of the world are available to them.

Who among us has not smiled as we watched *Alice, Tom Sawyer, Toad of Toad Hall, Mafutu,* or *Manolo* work their special brand of magic from the printed page? Who among us has not had that special magic worked on him? This creative interaction between the reader and print truly exercises what Shakespeare termed "the mind's eye." It is a wonder to behold.

What does *Cinderella* really look like? How does the Emperor in Hans Christian Andersen's *The Emperor's New Clothes* look? How can we describe *Rumplestiltskin?* What about the setting for each of these stories? How do we *know* what these characters and the environs they live in are like? One obvious way to know is to study the fine illustrations that accompany many of these old tales. In many versions, the illustrations are explicit as well as imaginative. They clearly give us enough pictorial information for us to build the imaginative structure that gives the story real meaning. However, another version may give us an entirely different view of a character or an environment. In one version, *Rumplestiltskin* is seen as an old elf, dressed in green, and fingering a long white beard as he bargains with the maid. Another version may show him as a dwarf, dressed in red with no beard at all. Likewise the maid is different, the room in the castle is of another design, and the medium the artist uses creates another mood. The same differences can be true of *Cinderella* or any of the old tales that have been produced in several editions.

The truth is, of course, that *Rumplestiltskin* and the maid, *Cinderella,* and all the rest, look the way the artist and the reader want them to look. There are, of course, some limitations on the creative venture but by and large, the illustrators see the characters and settings in their own way. That illustrations vary in their concept of how a tale should be pictured gives children an excellent chance to understand the value of the divergent thinking process of the creative person. There is no one correct way to imagine these characters. Youngsters will have favorite illustrators and will enjoy imagining with them the characters of a tale. They can compare and contrast, notice style and design, accept and reject. Many times, they prefer to create their own ideas of how the story should be illustrated. That they have the opportunity to know that there is no one way nor one image that is necessarily correct in the illustration of a tale, and that artists see these characters and the stories that house them in different ways, is an important step in accepting and understanding the value of divergent, creative thinking.

The children's trade book that is not a picture book, or a lavishly illustrated story, offers children another opportunity to exercise that creative, divergent quality they all possess. These books, usually for the middle or upper grades, give the youngster a real chance to create in his "mind's eye" the characters and the environment of the story and to develop an empathic response that puts him "into the story" so that he receives an emotional experience from the book. The authors of these books do paint a word picture for the reader. The picture they paint, however, is still made up of words on paper, nothing more.

The sketches in Joseph Krumgold's ... and Now Miguel scarcely give the reader a clear understanding of the characters and the setting in the sheep country of New Mexico. The imagery is built with words. The ominous sea and the looming ships in Howard Pease's The Black Tanker are there only in words, as are the characters. Aunt Polly's house and Jackson Island where Tom Sawyer romped are never clearly defined in illustration. They are seen through the brilliant writing of Mark Twain. The city streets and neighborhoods so clearly seen in Frank Bonham's Durango Street are created by words, only slightly aided by sketches. The artistry of language and the ability of an author to use it build the images and responses in the reader's mind. It is a mutually creative phenomenon. The author suggests through words what the reader completes through imagination.

What the child imagines as he interacts with the language of literature is a highly personal thing. He creates from what the author gives him. He develops his own images, his own pictures, his own version of the setting. Other children will vary from his ideas. They, many times, will disagree sharply about how a certain character or setting should look. Different responses from the same stimulus is clearly evident when children discuss their literature. Creative, divergent thinking is evident when children interpret what they read.

It is delightful to hear children respond to a movie version of a favorite book. They are frequently horrified at the liberty the Hollywood people take with their literature. The Walt Disney versions of some of the children's classics often leave children confused and unhappy. The writer remembers one little girl of ten who huffily reported to the class her reaction to Disney's *Mary Poppins*. "It wasn't *Mary Poppins* at all," she reported. "I don't even think she (the actress who played the title role) read the book!" Several fifth graders who saw the Disney version of *The Jungle Book* reported that surely the only thing Mr. Disney used in the film was the title. The teacher was reading the Kipling original to her class when the film came to the local theatre. The children attended the movie with real anticipation but came away disillusioned and more than a little unhappy. Children do not like their imaginative creations tampered with. When the plot line is changed, too, their reaction is often one of indignation.

Even when the film version of a children's book is done with taste and care, the youngster who knows the book, and has created his own imaginative construction of characters and setting, is sometimes unhappy with another's interpretation. The characters, the setting and the story are his. He helped to create them. A youngster is often jarred when someone else presents a different interpretation.

Scott O'Dell's wonderful *Island of the Blue Dolphins* was given screen treatment several years ago. It was done well, with care for the original story and its intent. As a film version of a children's book, it was head and shoulders above most attempts.

Yet, children's reactions to the film were mixed. One sixth grade boy openly rejected the film because the actress who played the role of Karana did not match his idea of the character. He frankly liked his version of her better. His version, of course, was built from the art of words on paper, a few sketched illustrations, and a creative imagination. That combination is a difficult one to beat.

Poetry is especially fine for the exercise of the creative imagination of children. A descriptive poem, whose words sing of image and rhyme, seldom fails to set young creative imaginations spinning. The poet, that special person, weaves words and sounds into a net that is designed to catch the imagination. Poetry is, of course, best when it is heard. The sound of poetry is a major factor in appreciating its beauty. The teacher who is skillful in the reading of poems, and is knowledgeable about poetry for children, can evoke responses from children that will be thrilling and most rewarding. The child who has had "visions of sugar plums dancing in his head" is lucky, indeed. They most often dance because of a poem.

Planned opportunities for divergent, creative thinking needs to be a part of regular classroom procedure. We know that the creative potential the child has can be encouraged and developed if correct environmental factors are present. Children's literature and regular opportunities to interact with it are an important part of that environment. There are few ways to stimulate creative thinking more effectively than with children's literature. Creativity is an intrinsic part of children's literature. We, as teachers, need to foster opportunities for its effect on our children.

## CHILDREN'S LITERATURE AS A SPRINGBOARD
### FOR CREATIVE ACTIVITY

Children's literature provides an excellent springboard for many different creative activities. The creative teacher who is aware of the possibilities literature provides for these activities could most likely fill an entire book with suggestions. Children's literature provides an almost bottomless well of ideas for an activity program.

The ideas that were offered in Section One of this book give some idea about the scope children's literature provides for creative activity in the various curricular areas. The children's trade book is a source, indeed a genesis for many creative projects in science, the arts, social studies, and the language arts. That children's literature, in that context, is able to undergird the curriculum, is obvious.

*Creative writing* is one activity that grows naturally from rich experiences with children's literature. When children are exposed to excellent models of language use, it follows that their own language will improve. Certain passages, descriptive sentences and phrases, or the effective use of a particular literary technique, such as onomatopoeia, can be brought to the attention of the young writer. Without overemphasizing the mechanics of these sections in their literature, the teacher can discuss with the class why such selections are effective. How did the author use words to make that passage or phrase as effective as he did? Did he bring the senses into play? What kinds of sentences did he use? What exciting words did he employ? Could the same passage be written in another way and would it be as beautiful or as exciting?

With the passages and the discussion of them fresh in mind, the teacher may then offer the youngster a chance to construct his own paragraphs and passages. One concept that can aid youngsters in the understanding of creative writing is that a writer uses techniques and special ways of working with words and phrases to build his thought. These ways of working with the language are his tools. These tools can be used by anyone who writes. The writer knows when to use the various tools so that he can better communicate his ideas.

The connotative power of writing can also be brought to the attention of the young writer. The same subject can be seen from many viewpoints and with various effects. The cat, for example, is a favorite subject of authors who write for children. How the author, aided by the illustrator, views the cat in the context of the story can vary greatly. The cat can be the dandy of *Puss in Boots* or the sturdy friend in *Dick Whittington and His Cat*

(Marsha Brown's versions emphasize this difference so well in illustration). She can be the dangerous huntress of John Langstaff's and Teodor Rojankovsky's *Frog Went A-Courtin'*, the wise cat of the back streets in Will's and Nicolas' *The Two Reds*, or the sleek, satisfied cat found in Beatrix Potter's *Peter Rabbit* books. Other cats are found in other books that give still other visions of how we view her. The author's craft lets us view the same subject in different ways. Children enjoy this; they enjoy taking opposing viewpoints on a subject. They find it delightful to use words to support their point of view. A creative writing experience, after viewing the many divergent ways that authors present their concept of a particular subject, might be a valuable opportunity for learning. Continuing with the cat as an example, the creative experience of writing two paragraphs about the cat, from opposing points of view, could be a rewarding, fruitful lesson in the language arts. Opposing points of view in words, phrases, and sentences can be an effective way of expression. That concept is one we all seek to develop in the language arts.

Children enjoy the creative experience of writing poetry. From the simple rhyme by the primary child to the longer, involved poem by the youngster in junior high school, the writing of poetry is an activity that appeals to many children. They enjoy using words in the poetic form; it is different, novel, beautiful, and effective.

As elementary teachers, we should not expect children to analyze the scheme or meter patterns of poetry. This concept is too advanced and should be left to the English teachers of high school and college. We can, however, offer children a wealth of poetry to enjoy and to serve as models for their writing. Poetry anthologies are easily accessible to teachers. Poems about holidays, weather, special events and poems that are valuable for their beauty of language and thought are available in abundance to children. We, as elementary teachers, need to provide our youngsters with many poetic experiences if we are to encourage our children to write poetry. We all need models to serve as examples in any endeavor. The young poet needs models, too, if he is to try his hand at writing poetry.

*The puppet theatre* is a natural activity that can grow from rich experiences with children's literature. The dramatizing of stories has appealed to children for hundreds of years. The drama is one of our oldest forms of literature.

The creative teacher, with a simple puppet theatre, a few basic hand puppets, a tape recorder, and a phonograph can start children on a highly creative, satisfying activity. A dramatized story, recorded by children on tape, can serve as the basic element in puppet theatre production. A tape recording can be as simple or as sophisticated as the class and teacher desire. It can have background music, provided by a phonograph and sound effects. A unit on puppetry can produce such activities as script-writing, set construction, costume making, and a host of related activities. It can, however, be as simple as retelling a favorite story in extemporaneous dramatic form. Some puppet theatres have been successful enough to go "on the road" to other classrooms in the building and to provide recess entertainment for groups of children during inclement weather. This activity, springing from literature for children, abounds with possibilities. The creative teacher can take her class to creative heights with puppet theatre activity.

The Roller Movie is another creative activity that can accompany or follow experiences with children's literature. The roller movie is a device that is familiar to most elementary teachers. It consists of a wooden frame, much like a picture frame, with two wooden rollers connected to the inside of the frame on opposite sides. Each of these rollers has a crank or other device that will allow it to be turned. The rollers hold paper that stretches across the inside of the frame. When one roller is cranked, the paper moves across the frame and is wound on the receiving roller.

The rolled paper in a roller movie is usually a type of paper used by butchers. It needs to be of sufficient length so that it will take several minutes to move across the frame from one roller to the other.

One activity that children enjoy is illustrating a favorite story and placing the illustrations on a roller movie for presentation. These illustrations can be done separately and glued to the paper roll or they can be drawn directly on the paper roll and be immediately ready for sharing. Children's concepts of characters, setting, and mood can be expressed easily on a roller movie. The possibilities for book reports, sharing favorite books, featuring new books, works of favorite authors, and concepts of informational books are easily seen.

The roller movie is a favorite visual aid of the primary teacher. Its use in the upper grades has unlimited possibilities, too.

*Dramatic play or creative drama* is another creative activity that springs naturally from experiences with children's literature. The fun and creative excitement of pretending a story, or part of a story, is difficult to equal. The comments and directions concerning dramatic play in Chapter IV of this book can be reviewed for more information about this very creative, valuable activity and its relationship to literature for children.

*Mural painting* is always a favorite activity of children. These large composites of pictures, cutouts, paintings, and drawings seldom fail to capture the imagination and interest of children. The mural depicting favorite children's books, characters or settings is a delight to see and is wonderful to watch as it develops. Each youngster has a favorite he wants included in the mural. How he goes about placing his contribution in the design of the mural is often a real exercise in creative problem solving. As a way of creating interest in books, the literature mural has few peers.

A complete list of creative activities that can result from children's experiences with their literature is a task that would fill several volumes and still be incomplete. Any attempt to compile such a list would be impossible. It may also seem patronizing on the part of the author to assume that the professional teacher lacks ideas of her own. This, of course, is not true.

Some suggestions have been offered as activities that lend themselves especially well to creative work on the part of students and teachers in relation to children's literature. Others are noticeably missing. What teacher is not aware of the value and creative possibilities found in verse choir or choral speaking, diorama construction, bulletin board design, box theatres, finger plays, peep boxes, clay modeling, writing to favorite authors, flannel boards, storytelling, compiling book lists, book fairs, and the like?

These learning activities are the familiar tools of all good teachers. That they can be employed in the literature program is obvious. The creative potential is inherent in them when combined with children and their literature.

## *Summary*

ALL CHILDREN HAVE CREATIVE POTENTIAL. It is our job as teachers to encourage and develop the creativity that all children possess. As educators, one way we can help this creative potential develop is to provide an environment that is conducive to creative and divergent thinking.

The literary environment we provide for our students can be most beneficial in helping develop the creative potential in all students. Literature for children depends upon the imagination and creativity of the reader. It provides opportunities to create a character, setting, and mood in the "mind's eye" of the reader. The words in print, through the magic of imagination, become a world of imagery. That, in itself, is a major creative achievement.

The creative activity that comes as a result of interaction with children's books provides many opportunities to exercise the creative, divergent thinking process. Creative writing, both in prose and poetry, is greatly enhanced if good literature is available to youngsters. The puppet theatre, dramatic play, the mural, and a host of related activities can result from a rich literary environment. Each activity enhances the literature program and provides creative opportunities that otherwise would be lacking.

The teacher who will concern herself with the development of the creative potential in youngsters will concern herself with literature for children. There are few ways to better enhance the creative abilities of children than with creative utilization of children's literature.

# EXERCISES
## FOR THE TEACHER

1.   Read a story to children. Discuss the characters, the setting, the times, etc., with them. Note how divergent, creative thinking results. Do they see the characters, etc. in the same way?

2.   What has been your reaction to a film based on a favorite book of yours? Do you always agree with how the film depicts what you have built as a mental image? Discuss this same phenomenon with children.

3.   If possible, develop a creative writing experience for children using good children's literature as its genesis.

4.   Examine several picture books that explore the same type of environment. Note how each artist sees the environment and thus presents it in a different way.

5.   In one of the many fine craft books available to you, note how a "roller movie" or puppet theatre is made. Construct one and offer a presentation to your class.

6.   Make a mural using children's literature as the central theme.

7.   Find, in various children's books, the way authors view different subjects. Read these to your class and discuss how the author used words to make his feelings clear.

8.   Listen to a recording of a children's story. How is interpretation of the story helped and hindered by the recording?

9.   Note the toy section of any department store. How is imagination and creativity being helped or hindered here? Compare the toys and their role in the development of creativity to good children's literature?

# SUGGESTED READINGS

CARLSON, RUTH K. "Stimulating Creativity in Children and Youth," *Elementary English*, XXXIX (1961), pp. 165–169.

CHAMBERS, DEWEY W. "Dramatic Play: A Magic Carpet to Learning," *California English Journal*, Vol. 2, No. 2 (Fall, 1966), pp. 60–64.

————. "Sign Posts to Creative Teaching," *The Instructor* (October, 1968).

DUFF, ANNIS. *Longer Flight*. New York: The Viking Press, Inc., 1956.

MARKSBERRY, MARY LEE. *Foundation of Creativity*. New York: Harper and Row Publishers, 1963.

MIEL, ALICE, ed. *Creativity in Teaching: Invitations and Instances*. Belmont, Calif.: Wadsworth Publishing Company, Inc., 1961.

SAWYER, RUTH. *The Way of the Storyteller*. Rev. ed. New York: The Viking Press, Inc., 1962.

SMITH, JAMES A. *Setting Conditions for Creative Teaching in the Elementary School*. Boston: Allyn and Bacon, Inc., 1966.

TORRANCE, E. P. *Guiding Creative Talent*. Englewood Cliffs, N.J.: Prentice-Hall, Inc., 1962.

————. *Rewarding Creative Behavior*. Englewood Cliffs, N.J.: Prentice-Hall, Inc., 1965.

WILT, M. *Creativity in the Elementary School*. New York: Appleton-Century-Crofts, Inc., 1959.

SECTION THREE

*Thoughts on Some Controversial
Issues in Children's Literature*

## Chapter VII

# SPECIAL ISSUES IN
# CHILDREN'S LITERATURE

*Children's literature,*
like any exciting and growing field, has issues and problems that
prove to be both knotty and controversial. These issues are
apparent whenever teachers, librarians, school officials, and
specialists in the area of children's literature meet. Many of these
issues are controversial because the problems they present are value
based and the solutions to them are open to debate. Others are
often not clearly defined and as such do not lend themselves to
well-thought-out solutions.

The special issues identified in the following section were
selected as those that appear to be most often discussed by
practicing teachers when they meet to consider literature for
children. The comments about these issues are written from a
point of view designed to stimulate thought and discussion. The
solutions to the problems these issues present are rightfully the
prerogative of the teacher and the school in which the issue is
identified. The points of view offered in the following pages will
hopefully aid the teacher and other educators toward successful
identification, and offer solutions to problems these special issues
present.

## The Modern "Chapbook"

THE "CHAPBOOK" is a seventeenth and eighteenth century English dialectic·term that in the modern vernacular would read "cheapbook." The little chapbooks were a form of literature offered by the pedlar of that period along with other trinkets and wares to those who would buy. The chapbook had from sixteen to sixty-four pages, often merely folded together, and sold for as little as a penny. Its content was usually made up of old legends, old tales from the Middle Ages, bits and pieces of fairy tales, hero stories, or just about anything that was available. The writers of these chapbooks condensed these tales down to their bare essentials —to save space and expense. In the condensation of these stories most of the charm was lost. The writing was bad, the grammar was often incorrect, and any illustrations they contained were poorly conceived and reproduced. Excitement, high action, and adventure were the keynotes of the chapbook. Literary quality was sacrificed for format and sales.

Though not exclusively written for children, the chapbook became a highly popular form of literature for children among the common folk of England at that time. The educated upper class very likely frowned upon the content and quality of these chapbooks but that did not affect their sales. They were eagerly purchased by both adults and children due in part to their low price and availability. They very likely were the first mass-produced bits of literary junk for children.

Though the chapbook, as it was originally known, has disappeared from the children's literary market, its descendents have thrived. The concept of a cheaply constructed, poorly written, badly illustrated book for children, sometimes a curious phenomenon that is not a book at all but a toy masquerading as a book, is a concept that is all too familiar.

The modern chapbook is easily seen as one walks along the aisles of some department stores, toy stores, supermarkets, and drug stores. Noticeable among the offerings will be the "popular" books for children. Displayed will be the horrendous Disney versions of the classics, Shirley Temple's saccharine and badly written folktales, the Roy Rogers syndrome, Soupy Sales, and even one where Jerry Lewis tells his favorite jokes. Sprinkled among these popular books will likely be several volumes concerned with *Batman* or the *Green Hornet*.

Next, gleaming in plastic coated cardboard, are the "cheapie" books, cranked out in untold millions and geared to the impulse buyer. These little books offer a diet of gaudy blandness. These are the "Happy Puppy Books," the "Trip to Grandma's for Cookies Books," the "Fuzzy Bunny Books." All are badly written, badly illustrated, and poorly bound. They sell for under a dollar and are worth much less.

Another eye-catching display is likely to be the books that do not need reading. These are the "Toy Books." Here we find a book that when opened becomes a three-dimensional Bavarian village, a circus tent with a bobbing clown, or a sailboat wiggling over a wavy sea. It is in this display that we find a book that when cranked plays music or when the string is pulled talks to us in a wispy, pseudo-child's voice. Here we find *Dr. Dan the Band Aid Man*, featuring a real band aid, or *Lolly, the Lollipop Girl*, replete with a colorful lollipop clinging to the cover. Others in this category are the terry-cloth books to wash with, the punch-out books promising paper dolls when the book is opened, and a whole array of gimmicks guaranteed to make appreciators of literature wince. These books are not books at all. They are toys. Why they must masquerade as books is another mystery of modern merchandising.

In this category, too, are the comics. While a comic book cannot be truly considered children's literature, as defined in this text, it may fall under the general heading of *The Modern "Chapbook."* They are inexpensive, available, and offer a starvation diet if they are the sole literary fare consumed by children.

The naive adult, the buyer of this material, is likely to don an indulgent smile and wonder at the fuss. After all they are kind of cute and they are just for the kids! We, as teachers, know that there is the rub. They *are* just for the kids. They may well be the first contact children have with books. They are likely to be factors in helping children understand the world of literature. They can be an important source in developing literary taste. Yet, literary "pap" of this kind in sufficient doses can stunt the development of literary appreciation. At best they can warp the child's concept of what a book is and the magic of the printed word. Attitudes toward books develop in childhood. For this reason, literary fare for children should be of the very best quality available.

As educators, we know that the very best is available in children's literature. Sometimes it takes a bit of searching to find it, but it is there. Amid the junk, the jewels glow. With over 2,000 new titles published each year in the children's book field, finding just the right book for a special child is a treasure hunt that can be both frustrating and delightful.

Children's books are an investment. The bringing together of a child and the right book is often the beginning of a long and valuable friendship—a friendship that can expand and grow in the realization that books can be a part of life. It is a long-term investment where interest can affect the reading habits of a lifetime.

A child's book is not a gimmick or a toy. It is not meant to dance or sing or be pulled apart to make a family of paper dolls. It is meant to give to the child the delight and magic of the printed word and the wonder of the art of illustration. In short, a child's book, like any other book, is meant to be read.

These modern chapbooks are obviously abundant. The sales volume, we are told, is fantastic. Some publishing houses exist upon the revenue secured from the sale of this material alone. No matter how we, as educators, may wish it, this material will not disappear from the shelves. The issue then is, what will we, as teachers, do about this material?

It is obvious that children are going to have this kind of material read to them, or will read it themselves from time to time. They come into contact with these books long before they come to school. Most toy boxes found in the home will contain several of these cheapbooks and many family libraries will count some of them among their collection.

The classroom is a carefully planned educational environment. It is a place where children come to learn under the guidance of a qualified teacher. The classroom is designed to provide children with the best the community can afford in terms of educational advantages. The classroom provides children with new and valuable experiences—experiences that are geared to broaden their horizon and extend their level of understanding. One of the experiences that the classroom must provide for children is a rich interaction with good children's literature—children's literature that can and will enhance the lives of those youngsters who interact with it.

The classroom is a standard setter also. It needs to represent that which is valuable and has quality. Certainly, this must be true in terms of children's trade books. Children appreciate quality if they are exposed to it. They very quickly understand the difference between the cheapbook and a children's book of substance and quality. Their experiences in the classroom literary environment should provide opportunities for them to make this distinction.

Certainly no classroom collection of books has room for the "cheapbook." It has no room for the book that is used as a toy. It has no room for a book that is not an excellent example of the best writing and illustrating available to children.

As teachers of the young, many times we have the opportunity to confer with parents about the welfare of their children. Many times parents come to us seeking advice about how they can undergird the child's education at home. The child's reading habits are often a point of discussion. At this time, the teacher can help the parent understand the necessity for quality in the reading material that children receive. We, as teachers, can point out that one trade book of real quality is worth many cheapbooks. We can help them understand that a good children's book will have qualities in the bookmaking format that will assure its lasting through reading after reading. A quality trade book requires a greater monetary investment than does the cheapbook, but the investment is a wise one. Quality and serviceability are what the investment brings. For the little difference in price, the returns are more than bountiful.

As teachers, we cannot, or should not, act as censors concerning what children read outside of school. We can, however, provide a rich literary environment for them at school and invite their interaction with it. With this interaction comes comparison. This is, of course, what we seek. It is a rare instance, indeed, when the literary junk found in the modern chapbook does not suffer greatly when compared to children's literature of real quality.

The modern chapbook is a part of our mass media. It is created and merchandised on a gigantic scale. Like all mass media, it is a part of the lives of children. It is, however, only a part. The modern chapbook can operate at an amazingly inefficient level in its effect on children if it is forced to compete with that which is good. And there is so much in children's literature that can offer real competition for the attention of the young reader.

## The Book Report

MOST TEACHERS seem to find it necessary for children to report to them about their recreational reading. They believe, and rightfully so, that if the teacher is to help children expand their literary education, they must know about the youngster and the books he chooses. This practice not only keeps the teacher informed about the reading habits of the youngster but also places emphasis on recreational reading and its role in the curriculum. A record of what a youngster reads is absolutely necessary if the teacher is to guide and encourage youngsters toward a rich literary experience in the elementary school.

The book report is a traditional educational tool. It has existed, presumably, ever since the trade book became a part of the educational environment. In its traditional form, however, the book report has probably done more to destroy the love of reading and the joy of books than any other single educational practice.

The book report, in its traditional form, consisted of a series of mimeographed questions about the book that the youngster was required to read. In addition, the form usually required a complete bibliographic statement and the number of pages in the book. The form often asked the youngster to define the type of book it was: Was it an adventure, a mystery, a humorous book, fiction, non-fiction, poetry? (The possibility of a book being a fictional mystery of high adventure with a great deal of humor involved in the story never seemed to occur to those who prepared these forms.) Most of these book report forms required a youngster to identify his favorite character (never more than one), his favorite part (assuming he could not have enjoyed the whole book), whether he would recommend the book to a friend (never bothering to ask why), and the like. Most often, there would be space at the bottom of the form on which the youngster was directed to tell about the book, most often its plot. This, of course, was required to be done in something like two paragraphs—a remarkable feat.

This rigid, unproductive way of reporting that a book was read was often accompanied by other requirements. Some teachers actually insisted that a certain number of books be read in order to receive an acceptable grade. Six books read and reported on in the manner described, for instance, might mean a grade of "C." Double that number and a student would receive a grade of "B," and so on.

This practice is no longer followed. The modern educator knows that this kind of rigid, constricting requirements often produce negative results. The modern teacher knows that this kind of requirement will reward the good reader and punish the youngster who, for one reason or another, is not reading with the necessary facility to meet this requirement. This kind of practice will often force children into dishonest acts to meet the requirements. Some children fearing failure will meet the book report requirements by simply filling out the form and neglecting to read the book. It is an unfortunate event when school requirements force a child to be dishonest to survive.

Certainly, the traditional book report which requires a specific number of books to be read will produce negative results in terms of attitude toward the trade book and literature. It takes recreational reading from the realm of enjoyment and puts it in the category of another imposed task which must be met. This kind of book reporting will likely ruin more potential readers of books than any practice we may have in education.

Yet, as teachers, we must know what books our students are reading and what their reaction is to these books if we are going to foster their literary development. Book reporting is needed. The issue is, how best can we facilitate this necessity?

One way, perhaps, to provide for book reporting, yet remove the stigma of the traditional book report, would be to change the semantic structure of this necessity. Perhaps rather than use the term book report, we could ask our students to keep a book list with a record of a short reaction to the books they have read. These book list forms can be created by the teacher or they can be secured from professional sources. Some of the better sources are:

1. *Books I Have Read.* Syracuse, New York: Gaylord Brothers, Inc.
2. Newton, H. C. *Reading Guidance Book.* Syracuse, N.Y.: The Bardeen Press.
3. Plybon, Louise. *Rainbow Reading Record.* Winston-Salem, N.C.: Bradford Printing Service.
4. Simpson, G. G. *My Reading Design.* North Manchester, Ind.: Reading Circle, Inc.

These devices, or one that the teacher constructs, can be a helpful way of keeping records of the children's reading habits.

Needless to say, more than a reading record is desirable in a literary curriculum. We want our youngsters to do more than just keep a record of what they read and their comments on their selections. We would hope that we might elicit a response from children about their reading in greater depth. How do they feel about the book? Why do they like it? Would they recommend it to others, and why? Children often become excited about a particular book; this excitement should not be ignored or lost.

Many creative teachers achieve this depth in response to literature by replacing the traditional book report with a technique some call book sharing. It does not necessarily carry any particular format or the number of books to be shared. Time is set aside periodically and facilities are made available to permit the sharing of books.

This sharing of books places an emphasis on oral communication and/or creativity. It often becomes a time not only of sharing but of selling a book to those who have not read it. Many times youngsters become so excited about a particular selection that they very much want others to have the same experience they have had. The sharing time often becomes a time to convince. There are few better ways of whetting the reading appetite than peer-to-peer dialogue about books. Not only does the student get the valuable experience of sharing his book with others, but the literary environment is enlivened, as well. A youngster, convinced of the value of a good trade book, and given the opportunity to say so to his peer group, is worth many, many visits by a professional librarian and talks by the teacher.

The techniques of book sharing are many and varied. One supposes there are as many techniques as the creative teacher can devise. Often a youngster or group of youngsters will move from a specific book to a group of books or to an author or illustrator as a focal point for discussion or presentation.

Listed here are a few ideas about book sharing. Each suggestion should trigger new, and perhaps better ideas, in the mind of the creative teacher. Each class or group of children is unique. The practice we employ to help them should be equally unique. Some suggestions that might offer fruitful expression are:

1.  Make a listening post. On a tape recorder have children comment on a recent book they have read. Change the tape every two weeks.
2.  Choose a favorite author or illustrator and give a brief account of his life. List his books.
3.  Locate the settings of regional stories or legends on a map. The map can be a library corner display. Children can discuss their favorite regional story using the map as a visual aid.
4.  Feature special kinds of books for a once-a-week discussion. Such categories as "Family Books," "Mystery Books," "Humorous Books," "Animal Stories," etc. can be featured in successive weeks. Children can share their favorite categories with each other during that time.
5.  Have children discuss what they think a certain author is like as he reveals himself in several books.
6.  Prepare an advertisement for a book and write a brief review of the book for the school or classroom newspaper.
7.  Write a television or radio script based upon a book or part of a book.

8. Create and tell riddles about a book, its plot, or characters.

9. Match titles of books with authors.

10. Have an imaginary interview with an author.

11. Prepare a series of clues to be used in identifying a book.

12. Construct a diorama or paint a mural representing a favorite book.

13. Make a series of illustrations for a favorite book. Discuss these illustrations with the class.

14. Create book jackets for favorite books.

15. Prepare oral reports to emphasize the relationship between the illustrations and the content of a book.

16. Illustrate a story through the use of puppets.

17. Make a crossword puzzle about a favorite book.

18. Make a pictured time line showing important points in a book. This technique is best for historical fiction or biography.

19. On a tape recorder present a dramatization of an incident in a favorite book. Use music, special effects, and dramatic expression. Play it to the class. Offer it to other classes.

20. Prepare and present a monologue from a favorite book.

21. Pantomime part of a story.

22. Make mobiles of important people and animals in a story.

23. When possible, compare the original form of a story with other versions of it as comics, rewritten versions, commercial film versions. Contrast the two forms.

24. Make a bulletin board of a favorite author and his books.

25. Make a bulletin board of favorite books.

26. Prepare a "This Is Your Life" program concerning a favorite character. Record it on tape.

27. Make a book list where children list five books that "everyone should read." *

Other creative ideas about how to help children share their books come from discussions educators have about books and

---

* Many suggestions listed are taken from ideas furnished by the teachers and supervisors of the Houston Independent School District, Houston, Texas.

children. These ideas need to be collected, preserved, and shared with other teachers.

It seems clear that, as teachers, we need to be aware of what children read and their reactions to what they have read. It is also clear that we can defeat our purpose if we move into this area with an instrument as rigid as the traditional book report. We need to seek and find ways to allow children to report their reading activities in ways that are as creative as the books they read.

## The Award Winners

THE CHILDREN'S BOOK FIELD is graced with many awards. Each year, certain children's books are, for one reason or another, singled out and made the recipient of a medal, a scroll, a check, or some other symbol of excellence. The competition for these awards is considerable. One result of these awards is, of course, a continued attempt at excellence by writers, illustrators, editors, and publishers of children's trade books. These awards provide a real service for children who read books. The books offered to them today are much superior to those offered in past years. This is due, in a large part, to recent attention given to the quality of children's books and manifested by the awards granted to them.

Many teachers who maintain a collection of trade books in the classroom rely upon the award winners as a criterion of excellence when they make their choices for the classroom collection. This practice is not an unwise one. The award winners are among the better children's books published each year. A teacher can rely upon award winners as a standard for excellence and by and large feel safe that they are correct.

To rely exclusively upon award winners, however, as a criterion for excellence in children's books is a limiting practice. Many fine children's books, books that have stood the test of time and are favorites of children, librarians, and teachers, have never been the recipient of an award. Many times award winners are less favorably reviewed and accepted by children and teachers than are those that fall into the runner up category.

To require the reading of the award winners is probably the poorest service a teacher can offer children. Some of these books, despite their excellence as acknowledged by adults, are not well accepted by children. Several winners of the more famous awards actually are not liked by children. Some of them present a reading level that most elementary school students find difficult. Even those award winners that are accepted by both children and adults are likely to suffer in their appeal if they appear on a required reading list. A teacher who is concerned about a good literary environment for youngsters will have award winners in her collection but will not rely upon them exclusively. There are many fine children's books available that have not won an award.

When a teacher includes award winners in a collection, she must know why the award was granted. Was the award given for literary excellence, or excellence in illustration? Is it a regional award, given to an author who lives in a certain geographic area? Is it an award given to a book that promotes kindness to animals? Is it one that is given to a children's book that emphasizes the concept of "one world"? What does the award mean and how does the recipient of the award meet the literary or curricular needs of that special group of children in a specific classroom? The variation of awards for children's books is considerable. These awards mean various things.

An example of the number of awards granted to children's books, as well as the variation of purposes for the awards, can be seen by the following brief description of some of the more important awards granted in the field of children's literature in the United States, Canada, and Great Britain.

*The Aurianne Award* □ ($200.00)

OFFERED BY:   The Children's Services Division
American Library Association
50 East Huron Street
Chicago, Illinois.

PURPOSE:   The purpose of the award is to develop humane attitudes toward animal life. The book must deal with animal life and be suitable for children from eight to fourteen years of age.

*Book-of-the-Year for Children Medal* □ (Bronze Medal)

OFFERED BY: The Canadian Library Association
Canadian Association of Children's Librarians
Room 606, 63 Sparke Street
Ottawa, Ontario, Canada.

PURPOSE: To encourage the writing and publishing in
Canada of good books for boys and girls by
Canadian authors. The book may be fiction or
nonfiction.

*Boys Life and Dodd, Mead Writing Award* □ (An inscribed
Medallion from Boys Life and the Boy Scouts of America.
Boys Life awards $1,250.00 for first serial rights; Dodd, Mead &
Co. awards $1,250.00 in advance against royalties)

OFFERED BY: Boys Life and Dodd, Mead & Co.
432 Fourth Avenue
New York, New York.

PURPOSE: The purpose of the award is to secure fine books
in the American tradition for young people. The
books are mainly written for boys.

*Brooklyn Community Woodward School Annual Award* □
($100.00 given to the United Nations International Children's
Emergency Fund in the name of the Author)

OFFERED BY: Brooklyn Community Woodward School
321 Clinton Avenue
Brooklyn, New York.

PURPOSE: The book must best interpret for children the
concept of One World.

*The Caldecott Medal* □ (Bronze Medal)

OFFERED BY: American Library Association
Children's Services Division
50 East Huron Street
Chicago, Illinois.

PURPOSE: To recognize the artist of the most distinguished
American picture book for children of the year.

*California Literature Medal Award* ☐ (Silver Medal)
OFFERED BY:   The Commonwealth Club of California
                 The Hotel St. Francis
                 San Francisco, California.
PURPOSE:   To encourage California children's authors to strive for excellence.

*Canadian Children's Book Award* ☐ ($1,000.00 and royalties from the sale of the book, as outlined in the contract)
OFFERED BY:   Little, Brown & Co. Boston and
                 Little, Brown & Co., Ltd.
                 25 Hollinger Road
                 Toronto 16, Ontario.
PURPOSE:   To select manuscripts from Canadian authors that are worthy of publication.

*The Carnegie Medal* ☐ (A Medal)
OFFERED BY:   The Library Association
                 Chaucer House, Malet Place
                 London W.C., England.
PURPOSE:   The award is given to raise the quality and standards of literature for children, to commemorate the centenary of the birth of Andrew Carnegie, and to bestow a hallmark of excellence upon the author.

*The Charles W. Follett Award* ☐ ($1,000.00, a Gold Medal, and $2,000.00 in advance against royalties)
OFFERED BY:   The Follett Publishing Company
                 1010 West Washington Boulevard
                 Chicago, Illinois.
PURPOSE:   To award an author of a children's book, above the picture book level, for his contribution to the field of children's literature.

*The Children's Book Award* ☐ (A Scroll)
OFFERED BY:   The Child Study Association of America, Inc.
                 132 East 74th Street
                 New York, New York.

PURPOSE:   The purpose of the award is to honor an author who, through his book, presents to children some of the real problems they are meeting in their world. Literary merit is of secondary importance.

*Children's Spring Book Festival Awards* □ ($200.00 each are given to the best three books in the categories of: picture books (for children ages four to eight), middle childhood books (ages eight to twelve), and older childhood books (ages twelve and up)

OFFERED BY:   The New York Herald Tribune
230 West 41st Street
New York, New York.

PURPOSE:   To encourage the spring publication of good books for children.

*Dorothy Canfield Fisher Children's Book Award* □ (A Scroll)

OFFERED BY:   Vermont Congress of Parents and Teachers and the Free Public Library Commission
Montpelier, Vermont.

PURPOSE:   To encourage Vermont children to read more and better books. It is designed to honor one of Vermont's most distinguished literary figures.

*The Follett Beginning to Read Award* □ (A Scroll and $2,000.00)

OFFERED BY:   The Follett Publishing Co.
1010 West Washington Boulevard
Chicago, Illinois.

PURPOSE:   The purpose of the award is to find the publisher suitable manuscripts of easy-to-read stories for the primary grades.

*The Franklin Watts Fiction Award* □ ($100.00 and $2,500.00 in advance against royalties)

OFFERED BY:   Franklin Watts, Inc.
575 Lexington Avenue
New York, New York.

PURPOSE: To award a distinguished contribution in fiction writing for children in grades three, four, and five.

*Indiana Authors Day Award* □ (A Certificate)

OFFERED BY: The Indiana University Writers' Conference
Ballingine Hall, Box 70
Bloomington, Indiana.

PURPOSE: The purpose is to honor the most distinguished children's book written in the past year by an author residing in Indiana.

*Jane Addams Children's Book Award* □ (A Certificate)

OFFERED BY: The Jane Addams Book Award Committee
for the Women's International League for Peace and Freedom
2006 Walnut Street
Philadelphia, Pennsylvania.

PURPOSE: The purpose is to encourage the publication of excellent books for children.

*Jewish Book Council of America Juvenile Book Awards* □ (A Citation and $250.00 in cash)

OFFERED BY: Jewish Book Council of America
15 East 26th Street
New York, New York.

PURPOSE: To encourage fine books for children that have a Jewish theme.

*Junior Book Awards* □ (Medals and Certificates)

OFFERED BY: Boys Clubs of America
381 Fourth Avenue
New York, New York.

PURPOSE: To encourage writing of quality books for boys from the ages of eight to sixteen.

*The Kate Greenaway Medal* ☐ (A Medal)

OFFERED BY: The Library Association
Chaucer House, Malet Place
London W.C., England.

PURPOSE: To honor the artist-illustrator of the most important picture book in the United Kingdom. The artist must be a British subject and domiciled in the United Kingdom. It is the British equivalent of the Caldecott Medal.

*The Laura Ingalls Wilder Award* ☐ (A Medal)

OFFERED BY: The American Library Association
Children's Services Division
50 East Huron Street
Chicago, Illinois.

PURPOSE: To honor authors and illustrators of American children's books in series form. The series needs to make a lasting contribution to children's literature.

*The Lewis Carroll Shelf Award* ☐ (A place on the shelf with *Alice in Wonderland* and other noteworthy books)

OFFERED BY: The University of Wisconsin School of Education and other cooperating state organizations, including:
The Wisconsin Free Library Commission
706 Williamson Street
Madison, Wisconsin.

PURPOSE: To encourage authors, publishers, parents, and librarians to compare contemporary children's books with *Alice in Wonderland*.

*The Librarian and Teacher Prize Competition* ☐ ($1,500.00 in advance against royalties and rights)

OFFERED BY: Dodd, Mead and Company
432 Fourth Avenue
New York, New York.

PURPOSE: To secure a book of high quality and establish the literary reputation of its author.

*The Nancy Block Memorial Award* □ (An Honorary Award and $25.00)

OFFERED BY: The Downtown Community School
235 East 11th Street
New York, New York.

PURPOSE: To foster intercultural relations among children through the books they read.

*National Mass Media Awards* □ ($250.00 and a Scroll)

OFFERED BY: The Thomas Alva Edison Foundation, Inc.
8 West 40th Street
New York, New York.

PURPOSE: The award seeks to contribute to the growth and development of children and serve as a source of inspiration to them. The award is given to the best science book of the year.

*The John Newbery Medal* □ (A Bronze Medal)

OFFERED BY: The American Library Association
Children's Services Division
50 East Huron Street
Chicago, Illinois.

PURPOSE: The John Newbery Medal is given to encourage original and creative work in the field of literature for children, to emphasize to the public that contributions to the literature for children deserve recognition as do poetry, plays, or novels; to give those librarians who make it their lifework to serve children's reading interests an opportunity to encourage good writing in this field. The author must be an American.

*The Ohioana Book Awards* □ (A Ceramic Medal)

OFFERED BY: The Martha Kinney Cooper Ohioana Library Assn.
1109 Ohio Departments Building
Columbus, Ohio.

PURPOSE: To honor Ohio writers, to acquaint the public with their works, and to collect these books in one place so as to preserve the cultures and traditions of Ohio.

*The Regina Medal* □ (A Medal)

OFFERED BY: The Catholic Library Association
Villanova University
Villanova, Pennsylvania.

PURPOSE: To encourage the professional in juvenile literature. Authors, publishers, illustrators, editors, etc. are eligible for this award.

*The Sequoyah Children's Book Award* □ (A Medal)

OFFERED BY: The Oklahoma Library Association, The Oklahoma Education Association, the State Department of Education, the Oklahoma State Library, Oklahoma Council of Teachers of English, Oklahoma Congress of Parents and Teachers, the University of Oklahoma Library School.

PURPOSE: To encourage American writers of children's books and to encourage Oklahoma children to read the best children's books available.

*The Seventeenth Summer Literary Award* □ ($250.00 and $1,000.00 against royalties, rights, and commissions)

OFFERED BY: Dodd, Mead & Co. and
Compact, The Teen Digest
432 Fourth Avenue
New York, New York.

PURPOSE: For the publisher to find novels of distinctive merit for young people.

*The Texas Institute of Letters Award* □ (The recipient receives $100.00 worth of books of his choice)

OFFERED BY: The Cokesbury Book Store
1910 Main Street
Dallas, Texas.

PURPOSE: To stimulate interest in Texas letters.

*Young Reader's Choice Award* □ (A Scroll)

OFFERED BY:   Pacific Northwest Library Association
Children's and Young People's Division
New Westminster Public Library
New Westminster, B.C., Canada.

PURPOSE:   To honor a book chosen by children and to center attention on books and reading. It is also designed to bring together librarians of the region.

*The William Allen White Children's Book Award* □ (A Bronze Medal)

OFFERED BY:   The William Allen White Library
Kansas State College
Emporia, Kansas.

PURPOSE:   To encourage Kansas children to read more and better books and to honor the memory of the state's most distinguished citizens.

# The Classics

THE CLASSICS in the children's field are among the most beloved pieces of literature in our culture. Their very names carry a special magic that is due only to a work of art that is worthy of the name *classic*. *Alice in Wonderland, Robin Hood, Tom Sawyer, Swiss Family Robinson, Treasure Island, Peter Rabbit, Little Women, Robinson Crusoe, Heidi*—the list is long and glittering. These children's tales are known and loved by generations of readers. They are the great books in the field of children's literature.

A classic in children's literature can be defined as a literary work of acknowledged excellence. It is a book that has outlived its author by several generations. It is a book of lasting merit.

The classics in children's literature have hallmarks. They become classics because of certain qualities they possess. They have, for instance, the ability to arrest and then hold the imagination of the reader. Once he becomes involved with the book, this quality is evident. He is reluctant to have it end and will often want to experience the book again and again. The children's classic tells a direct story. It moves from the exposition and the problem to the conclusion with the sureness of an arrow shot from a bow. It is uncluttered, clean in its execution, and true to its intent.

Another hallmark of a children's classic is the author's ability to communicate his sincerity. The person who interacts with a classic in the children's field knows that this is a book that *had* to be written. The author has an important, personal message to convey. It is guilelessness in its art, its truth speaks for its sincerity. The qualities of sincerity and honesty permeate the work. It was written because the author was compelled to do so and his love for the story is evident in his telling it.

A children's classic will also deal with issues that are timeless. The validity of *Robin Hood*'s exploits, the family solidarity of *Little Women*, the triumph of *Heidi*'s adventure over her environ-ment are as real and immediate today as they were when they were first written. This quality in a children's classic is one of the most important variables that keeps the book alive. It does not become dated, nor a period piece. It is as timely and as valid today as when it was written.

The element of humor is a major part of any children's classic. The humor, however, is at several levels. The most obvious, of course, is the broad humor that operates at the plot level. This humor is geared to the youngest and sometimes laces in a subtle, delicate shading that amuses the adult. It is often slapstick in its approach—humor that results in gales of laughter from the young reader for whom it was written. Other levels of humor in a children's classic are not so obvious, or so broad. The delicate humor of satire, for example, is often present behind this broad humor. The obvious humor that Twain included in *Tom Sawyer* concerning certain practices of the church of that day has behind it real satire aimed directly at the adult. The children's classic has, as a hallmark, humor that can be appreciated at several levels of maturity. That a person will read and re-read a children's classic over the years is not surprising.

Adventure, too, will operate at more than one level in a children's classic. The obvious is again at the plot level. The adventures of ideas, of philosophy, of man in his quest for his ideals often lie submerged just below the plot level of a strong hero and his adventure.

The characters in a children's classic are multidimensional creations. They most often are strong and heroic but possess the flaws and fallible qualities that are present in real people. They are understandable and they invite identification. A reader will often know more about himself, others, and the human species after he has interacted with the characters in a children's classic. The writers of these tales were often masters of human psychology as well as artists with the written word.

The most important hallmark of a children's classic is that the language used in telling the story is the finest our culture has to offer. It is well written, has a capturing style, possesses aesthetic qualities, and uses beautiful language. It is an excellent example of the art of literature. The plots of many classics are trite, unimaginative, and relatively unexciting. It is in the writing of these stories that the value lies. This variable, the excellence of writing, is the major hallmark of a children's piece of classic literature. Without this fine writing, the classic could not exist.

As teachers, we know the value of having children interact with the classics. We know that these fine books provide a common link between the generations. They are a part of our cultural heritage and are a part of our childhood education. We know that they provide an identification with the timelessness of basic issues and problems. They help children understand that the adventure of man is essentially the same regardless of the time culture in which he finds himself. And, as teachers, we know that these fine books offer children an experience with the finest writing in our culture. They provide experiences with literature for children at its height. They are valuable books, indeed. Every classroom collection should count some classics among its selections.

The question naturally arises about how to bring the classics and children together. What can we do, as teachers, to insure the literary heritage of our students? Should the classics be on a required reading list for children? Of course not. As indicated earlier, the dimension of required reading removes much of the joy of reading and thus much of the value. A sure way to turn children away from the classics is to attempt to force them into reading these books. For the most part, the classics of children's literature are difficult to read; the print barrier is too difficult for most elementary school students.

One way, and certainly a valid way, of bringing children and the classics of their literature together, despite the problems of reading difficulty for children, is to read the classics to them. These books lend themselves well to oral reading. The content of the classics is often very worthwhile to children long before they can actually read the text. One or two classics a year, alternated with other good selections of children's literature, read orally at the rate of a chapter a day, can bring children the thrill of great literature in a convenient, expeditious way. That twenty minutes or so spent in oral reading of the classics to children is time well invested.

It is best not to bring some classic literature to children too early. Most selections should not be offered to children, even in oral form, before the intermediate grades. Of course, like any general statement, there are notable exceptions to the generalization. The exceptions are, of course, left to the discretion and good taste of the teacher who serves as a literary guide to the children in her care.

There is an unfortunate product on the literary market that attempts to give children instant classic literature in a form that even the youngest can read. These products are usually termed "rewritten classics." It is their role to present a classic piece of children's literature, which is in the public domain, restructure and rewrite it so that it can fall comfortably into the reading vocabulary range of the middle or lower grades. Most children's classics have been on these literary surgical tables, and the results are horrendous.

Under these circumstances, the entire issue of why classic literature for children has become classic is lost or ignored. The plot of many of these stories is not worthy; it is the writing that clothes the plot that makes the difference. These rewritten classics are many times bland, are facsimilies of the original, and literary "pap," not worthy of the titles they carry.

These rewritten classics are openly dishonest. They masquerade as something they are not. Parents, and sometimes teachers, encourage children to read these products presumably as a way of achieving instant culture and predigested heritage. This kind of encouragement, of course, has its own reward: the acceptance of the pseudo as real. The sad part of this kind of practice is that if the youngster believes he has read *Tom Sawyer*, rewritten in words of no more than two syllables, he will never take the opportunity, nor seek it, to experience the magnificent original by Twain. He will be much the poorer for it, tricked out of the real experience by a false product.

Parents and teachers may argue that the rewritten classics provide readiness for the original. That is nonsense. If these people must get children ready for an experience with something as universally delightful as *Swiss Family Robinson*, and this book is best read to them in the middle grades, there are better ways of doing this than through a rewritten version of this wonderful adventure. Even the comic book version would be more acceptable than the rewritten version. At least the children would know they are not getting the original. The format of the classic comic books is not similar in appearance to that of a book, in the traditional sense. It would be difficult to confuse the original with the comic.

Not only do the classics come as rewritten, but are retold by someone in his own version. The most obvious practitioner of this activity is the Walt Disney Corporation. Its effort with the classics is disastrous. It is difficult to find a Disney version of a classic without molasses and theatrics running through a mutilated version of the story. The Disney versions are based upon his movie adaptations of the books. Heaven knows that the movies are bad enough—but to base a book on them and call them classic children's literature is enough to chill the blood.

Real children's classic literature remains as one of the special delights of childhood. The education of children is incomplete without an opportunity to know and interact with them. As teachers, it is our responsibility to bring children and classic literature together. It is a delightful responsibility. It demands, moreover, that we move with honesty and professionalism.

## The Paperback

MODERN PRODUCTION TECHNIQUES have, in the last decade, brought the paperback to the American reading public. The success of the paperback has been phenomenal. Their modest price and convenient format have brought book ownership well into the economic realm of all. To the publisher and the author, the paperback has meant a bonanza. To the reading public, it has meant numbers of books in the home that would not otherwise have been available. The paperback book has literally revolutionized the publishing industry. The paperback speaks clearly in the language of mass media. Its message is valuable and worth the time it takes to listen.

The children's literary field has also been affected by the paperback. Numbers of fine children's books, in paperback form, are available to the young reader. By and large, this is a good thing. It is good because children enjoy the ownership of books. They enjoy building a library so that they can read their favorites again and again. Children enjoy trading paperbacks with their friends and certainly the parents enjoy the small expense involved in helping children develop a personal library composed of paperback editions of good children's literature.

Most juvenile paperbacks are carefully produced to preserve the format of the original. This is a good idea especially for the picture book or in the children's book where the illustrations play an important role in telling the story. Many companies who produce children's books in paperback form (some call them "softback" or "softbound"; it means the same thing) actually utilize the original plates that were used when the book was first published. This assures the same format, illustrations, creative use of print, and framing that was used in the original. Many times they will reduce the size of the book, keep the format, and thus keep intact the style and intent of the original.

It is unfortunate when this is not done. A child's book that depends upon the format for its effectiveness is reduced to something it need not be. Of course, many juveniles written for older children do not depend upon illustrations in their format to make an effective presentation. These books, then, do not suffer in the least with a format different from the original.

Some companies are offering whole collections of children's

books in paperback, complete with cardboard display cases. These are usually a collection of children's books meant to be used as an "Individualized Reading Program" and come with a teacher's guide and other materials. They are valuable in a reading program, but of greater value is that a classroom can have an instant library collection in paperbacks at a fraction of the cost of the hardbound originals. Most of these collections are excellent in the selections they offer. *The Macmillan Reading Spectrum* is a notable, but not an exclusive, example of the paperback collections that are available, at a nominal cost, to schools. It is wise not to ignore their possibilities and potential.

Most children's librarians, school librarians, or committees involved in ordering books for a school or district tend not to order paperbacks when they make their final selections, however. They do so, not out of scorn or snob practice, but for a very practical reason. The paperback in children's literature, despite its lower cost, is not thought to be a good investment for a school district or a library if the book is to be in open circulation. The paperback will simply not withstand the use that children give it.

The bookmaking of a hardbound children's book is designed to let the book take the hard use that it will receive from young readers. The covers are usually made of firm cardboard, covered with a treated linen or other long wearing, stain and moisture-proof material that can be wiped clean. The book is held firmly between these covers by end pages that are glued to the cover. These end pages are made of strong paper that guarantees long wear. The pages of the book are also constructed to endure long wear.

Most hardbound children's books have their pages stitched together, in small page bundles, and then secured firmly to the end pages and to the cover itself. The probability of a lost page is extremely slight when the pages are sewn together in this manner.

This kind of bookmaking assures long wear. These hardbounds are, to use a descriptive phrase, relatively "kid proof." They are designed to be used by many children and with reasonable care will survive to be read and read again.

To be sure, the hardbounds are more expensive than the soft-bounds or paperbacks. The service they will render, however, more than makes up for the additional expense. A paperback children's book simply will not last as long and, therefore, cannot return its investment as well as a hardbound children's book where the investment is expected to serve as part of a public or school children's library collection.

The paperback in children's literature is an exciting, valuable addition to the field. The mere fact that the paperback makes good children's books available to more children is enough to justify its importance. The paperback does, however, have its limitations. While they serve the individual child through his personal library and a classroom as well, their service to a larger community of readers is limited because of its bookmaking and serviceability.

There is going to be an increase of paperbacks in the children's book field. More and more publishers are going to offer more books in this form. The market clearly shows that the paper-back sells well. Publishers have responsibilities to their stock-holders, and when a product sells well, we can assure ourselves it will continue to be offered. This is well and good. As teachers, we can expect our students to have a richer experience with their literature as a result.

To those who would examine what is available in paperback for children, the following are excellent sources:

1. Weber, Olga, ed. *Paperbound Books in Print.* New York: R. R. Bowker Co.

2. *Paperbound Book Guide for Elementary Schools.* New York: R. R. Bowker Co., 1967.

These useful reference sources, available in most public and university libraries, come in three cumulative issues per year. It provides the author, title, and name of the company that offers the book in paperback form.

The issue of the paperback in children's literature does not appear to be a question of "what" or "why," but rather of "how." How does one utilize this wealth of literature for children in an effective way? As personal or classroom copies, they offer great rewards. As part of a circulating collection meant for continued general use, they have limitations.

## The Series Books

THERE SEEMS TO BE A PHASE that most children go through that has them reading the series books. They read them one after another and look for more. The adventures of *Nancy Drew, The Bobbsey Twins, Mark Tidd, Sue Barton*—the list is long—all belong to that kind of children's literature that falls under the general heading called "The Books in Series." Children have read them for years, continue to read them today, and probably will read them in the future.

Most good children's library collections, or collections that belong to elementary schools, do not include the series books among their selections. They are excluded because there is general agreement among specialists in children's literature that these books are not good literature, or at least, not good enough to be included in school or public library collections. While this exclusion is probably justified, it does not seem to stem the flood of series books on the market, or to discourage children from reading them. Many of these books in series are basking in the enviable position of "best sellerism." They are inexpensive, readily available, and come in sets of numerous volumes that invite collection. They are favorite Christmas and birthday gifts from favorite aunts and uncles, who read them when they were children. Many times sets of these serials are passed from parent to child, and, therefore, have a patina that can be mistaken for classic.

Why are these series books considered less than good literature? What aspects of the serials are objectionable? In order to understand some of the basic points of argument against these books, it is necessary to examine them. It may be good to consider (*1*) the plots, (*2*) the characters, and (*3*) the language used.

THE PLOT. If we can generalize about the plot of the series books, we will find that most of the plots are extremely simple and predictable. The predictability of the plot borders on the stereotype. The same melodramatic structure is used again and again. The plot structure of the series depends upon action, excitement, adventure, and change. These elements of the plot often occur without development or motivation. Little or no credibility is given as to why this high action takes place. The stereotyped predictability of these plots is often a source of humor for the more sophisticated adult, particularly the university student, who describes the children's series books as "camp," meaning ostentatious nothingness.

The plot usually has a time setting of anytime, twentieth century. The plots are periodically updated, so that they fall comfortably into the contemporary. Likewise, the setting is often anyplace, U.S.A. We are never sure just what the geographic location is, except that a setting is often called "Centerville" or "Midtown." This is probably done so that the reader can imagine that Nancy Drew or any of the other heroic characters that exist in the series might live somewhere near the location of the reader.

The endings of these stories are notably inconclusive and are always predictably happy. There is seldom, if ever, a significant conclusion, an ending that can deepen a youngster's understanding of himself or the world in which he lives. They simply end, and the reader can move on to the next adventure.

These books do not need to be read in order. One may choose them at random. The characters do not grow, mature, or otherwise change. The many adventures of the hero or heroine seem to be frozen in time.

THE CHARACTERS. Most of the characters in the children's series fall into the stereotypes that one might expect after an examination of the plot. The hero or heroine of these tales is designed to fit the "All American" image. They are white and Anglo-Saxon. They are very much idealized. They possess great amounts of courage, intelligence, good looks, talent, stamina, and good luck. If they have faults, they are never revealed. The main character is impetuous; he often acts without thinking, but always successfully. His development, as a literary figure, is extremely shallow. We really do not know much about him; we only know what he does. In the series, there are one or two main characters or "stars." The supporting characters exist to complement the hero or heroine. Their development is even more shallow.

The hero or heroine is usually teen-aged. They do not grow up, they don't benefit from past experience, they simply remain teen-aged. How they support themselves, why they are not in school, where their parents are, all remain unknown.

The villain in the children's series books is equally stereotyped. He is every bit as bad as the hero is good. As the hero is Anglo-Saxon, the villain is dark, southern European, Latin, or Oriental. He is often oily and evil with no redeeming feature in his character. When he is thwarted, his trouncing is complete. He may show up again in a later adventure, but in the current adventure, at least, he is completely and absolutely defeated.

THE LANGUAGE. The most important element in literature, for children as well as adults, is the language used in the telling of the story. The artful use of language is the major hallmark of any piece of good literature. In the children's series books, good writing is a rare occurrence.

There is a sameness in the writing of these books. The vocabulary is easy to read and quite bland. There is little progression in vocabulary from easy, to more advanced, as the books progress from adventure to adventure. By and large the authors of these books use short, simple, declarative sentences throughout. Very little description is available to the youngster so that he can create with the writer a mutual experience as is found in good literature.

The language is repetitive in the series books. A favorite technique seems to be a heavy reliance on dialogue. Sometimes there are pages of dialogue to carry the story from one point to another, from one adventure to another. As literature, the children's series books leave much to be desired.

Why then, if the serials contain the weak points as outlined above, do they survive and flourish in the literary marketplace? Why are they so popular?

There are probably several reasons why these books in series continue to survive. First, and perhaps most importantly, these books are very easy and inexpensive to obtain. They are available not only in book stores but in toy stores, department stores, supermarkets, and the like. The entire set of a series is usually on display and several of them can be purchased for the price of one book of probably higher merit. Also, these books are easy to read. Children in the middle grades, for whom these books were written, can read them with real ease, and acquire a certain feeling of accomplishment in reading them so easily.

Many times middle grade youngsters read the series books for group reasons. They enjoy trading with one another or comparing how many books in a certain series they have read. Reading them becomes the fad and the proper thing to do to acquire status within a peer group.

Family interest in the series books is perhaps another reason why these books maintain their popularity. Many times sets of them that once belonged to a parent are passed on to the child. They are often given as gifts, also. The parent, or other adult, often is not knowledgeable about what is available in the area of children's literature and a selection from the books in series seems like a good gift idea.

Do we, as teachers, need to be greatly concerned about children reading the series books? Will their literary education be hindered by their interacting with these books? Probably not. Most youngsters who read the books in series wear them out and go on to other and better selections. It is probably not a good idea, however, to feature the series books in a classroom or library collection, as there are so many other fine books available which would benefit youngsters. Likewise, when children bring them from home and request that they be read orally, we should politely but firmly refuse, indicating that other books have been scheduled and that the series book is not a book that all children will enjoy.

It is dangerous and a bit presumptuous for us to refuse to have the series books in the classroom if children bring them. This kind of reaction is too strong and will likely send children underground. A good teacher, by her polite, friendly attitude of nonacceptance, can very likely put the books in series in a perspective that will render them unimportant.

A good teacher who finds youngsters involved with the series books can provide children's literature that will meet many of the needs found in these books as well as provide an experience with excellent literature. She can offer the *family chronicle*.

The family chronicle, like the series books, comes in a set of several volumes. They, however, tell in chronological fashion the story of a family. With emphasis on the lives of one or two members of the family the reader follows them from early childhood to adult life and old age. These books, to receive full benefit from them, must be read in order, not at random like the serials.

The family chronicle is best understood by those fortunate readers who have lived with Laura Ingalls Wilder in her magnificent chronicle, *The Little House Series*. This saga of a family begins with *The Little House in the Big Woods* which places the family in a Wisconsin wilderness cabin. The chronicle continues with *The Little House on the Prairie, On the Banks of Plum Creek,* and *By the Shores of Silver Lake* in which the family moves, grows, becomes older, and changes. The final book in the chronicle, *These Happy Golden Years,* finds the heroine, who was a young child in the first book, grown old and happy with her memories. She has had a full rich life, one that can be shared with the fortunate children who know these books.

The Laura Ingalls Wilder books, like other family chronicles, offer youngsters a chance to understand and interact with the various phases of life that these books portray. The characters are real, they have dimension, they can be understood. These books offer more than just a slick plot. They offer a level of psychological understanding and a symbolic message that lasts long after the book has been completed. These books are satisfying. They are substantial. They are good literature.

The books in series and the interest they generate in youngsters can be enhanced and furthered by the family chronicle. The family chronicle needs to be waiting on the shelves when the teacher notes that the series books have made their entrance into the reading lives of the children. While the series itself is probably not a harmful thing, a steady diet of them could result in literary starvation. A very good way to supplement the diet is with the literary nutrition supplied by the family chronicle.

## The Controlled Vocabulary

IN RECENT YEARS there has developed a curious hybrid in the children's literary field. It results from a union of the text and the trade book. It is called, for obvious reasons, "literature with a controlled vocabulary." Its purpose is to serve as a better way of helping children learn to read, to bring more enjoyment to the task of learning to read, and to encourage children to read more. The controlled vocabulary book very likely achieves its goal. They very well may serve teachers and students in the task of teaching and learning the skills of reading. Because of their ease, due to the control of the vocabulary they contain, children will likely read them and will feel a sense of accomplishment. It is very likely that these little books do what they are designed to do.

These controlled vocabulary books, or the "I can read it" syndrome that goes with them, however, should not be confused with children's literature. They simply are not children's literature and the person who confuses them with literature for children does a disservice to both literature and the controlled vocabulary books that brought about the confusion.

A children's trade book is a book of literary worth. It is to be used *by* children as a source of enjoyment and literary growth. Its primary purpose is to give pleasure aesthetically. Like any art form it can and does instruct but that is not its major purpose. Its major purpose is to delight children with the artful use of words and illustration.

The textbook, on the other hand, is meant to instruct. It is designed to be a teaching aid. It is, in a sense, designed to be used *on* children, rather than *by* them. Aesthetics and art, the delights of language and illustration, are often present in texts but are not necessary elements in them. Literary quality is of secondary importance in a text.

Children's literature and children's textbooks have two distinct roles in the lives of children. It is difficult to determine which has the more important role in the lives and education of children.

The controlled vocabulary book, while it purports to have qualities of both text and trade, really falls into the category of the text. Many will argue this point but one must ask the purpose of these books before he can determine in what category they belong. It is suggested here that these books have as their major purpose, the instruction of children and, therefore, do not belong in the realm of children's literature as described in this book.

The issue of the rewritten or easy reading classic has been discussed under the heading *The Classics* in this section. A further examination of this unfortunate practice does not belong in a consideration of the controlled vocabulary book.

The real issue of the controlled vocabulary book in the educational scheme of a child's experiences at school is not "shall they be used," but more "how shall they be used." They can serve a very useful purpose. They can very likely serve as an aid in helping children learn to read; they can make the task of learning to read more pleasurable; they can be read easily by most children; and they will likely give certain children a sense of accomplishment when they read them. That is all well and good. They should not, however, be a substitute for children's literature in the curriculum or the lives of children.

# BIBLIOGRAPHY

ADAMS, BESS P. *About Books and Children: Historical Survey of Children's Literature.* New York: Holt, Rinehart and Winston, Inc., 1953.

AMERICAN ASSOCIATION FOR THE UNITED NATIONS. *Read Your Way to World Understanding: A Selected Annotated Reading Guide of Books About the United Nations.* New York: Scarecrow Press, 1963.

AMERICAN LIBRARY ASSOCIATION. Children's Services Division. Book Reevaluation Committee. *Notable Children's Books, 1940–1959.* Chicago: ALA, 1966.
———. Special Committee of the National Congress of Parents and Teachers and the Children's Services Division. *Let's Read Together: Books for Family Enjoyment.* 2nd ed. Chicago: ALA, 1964.

ARBUTHNOT, MAY H. *Children's Books Too Good to Miss.* 5th ed. Cleveland: Press of Case-Western, 1966.

BAMMAN, HENRY A., AND WHITEHEAD, ROBERT. *Oral Interpretation of Children's Literature.* Dubuque, Iowa: Wm. C. Brown Company, 1964.

*A Basic Book Collection for Elementary Grades.* 7th ed. Chicago: ALA, 1960.

*Best Books for Children: A Catalog.* New York: R. R. Bowker, 1968.

*Books for Children, 1960–65.* Chicago: ALA Library, 1966–67.

CALIFORNIA ASSOCIATION OF SCHOOL LIBRARIANS. *Book List for Elementary School Libraries.* Edited by Margaret H. Miller. Santa Ana: Professional Library Service, 1966.

CANADIAN LIBRARY ASSOCIATION. Association Canadienne des Bibliotheques. *Basic Book List for Canadian Schools: Elementary Division, Grades 1–6.* Ottawa: 1966.
————. Supplement.

CHASE, JUDITH W. *Books to Build World Friendship: An Annotated Bibliography of Children's Books from Preschool to 8th Grade, Europe.* Dobbs Ferry, N. Y.: Oceana Publications, Inc., 1964.

*Children, Books and Reading.* Prepared by a Committee of the International Reading Association. Newark, Del.: International Reading Association, 1964.

COLBURN, EVANGELINE. *Books and Library Reading for Pupils of the Intermediate Grades.* Chicago: University of Chicago, 1942.

CUNDIFF, RUBY E., comp. *101 Plus Magazines for Schools, Grades 1–12.* 4th ed. Nashville, Tenn.: 1946.
————. *Recommended Reference Books for the Elementary School Library.* 2nd ed. Chicago: Wilcox and Follett, 1951.

DOBLER, LAVINIA G. *The Dobler World Dictionary of Youth Periodicals.* New York: Schulte Publishing Company, 1966.

EAKIN, MARY K., comp. *Good Books for Children: A Selection of Outstanding Children's Books Published, 1950–1965.* 3rd ed. Chicago: University of Chicago, 1966.

EATON, ANNE T. *Reading with Children.* New York: The Viking Press, Inc., 1952.
————. *Treasure for the Taking: A Book List for Boys and Girls.* Rev. ed. New York: The Viking Press, Inc., 1957.

*The Elementary School Library Collection, Phases 1–2–3.* Edited by Mary V. Gaver. 2nd ed. Newark, N. J.: Bro-Dart Foundation, 1966.

ENOCH PRATT FREE LIBRARY, Baltimore. Office of Work with Children. *Stories to Tell: A List of Stories with Annotations.* 5th ed. Baltimore, Md.: 1965.

FENNER, PHYLLIS R. *Something Shared, Children and Books: A Personal Treasury of Stories, Articles, and Cartoons.* New York: The John Day Company, Inc., 1959.

FISHER, MARGERY. *Intent Upon Reading: A Critical Appraisal of Modern Fiction for Children.* New York: Franklin Watts, Inc., 1962.

FRANK, JOSETTE. *Your Child's Reading Today.* Garden City, N. Y.: Doubleday and Company, Inc.. 1960.

GILLESPIE, JOHN, AND LEMBO, DIANA. *Juniorplots: A Book Talk Manual for Teachers and Librarians.* New York: R. R. Bowker, 1967.

GREEN, ROGER L. *Tellers of Tales: British Authors of Children's Books from 1800–1964. With a Chronological Table of Famous Children's Books to the Present Day, and Lists of Titles by Each Author.* New York: Franklin Watts, Inc., 1965.

HARRINGTON, MILDRED P. *The Southwest in Children's Books: A Bibliography.* Baton Rouge, La.: State Publishing Co., 1952.

HORN, THOMAS D. *Books for the Partially Sighted Child.* Champaign, Ill.: National Council of Teachers of English, 1965.

THE HORN BOOK MAGAZINE. *A Horn Book Sampler on Children's Books and Reading: Selected from Twenty-five Years of The Horn Book Magazine, 1924–1948.* Edited by Norma R. Fryatt. Boston: The Horn Book, 1959.

HUBER, MIRIAM B., ed. *Story and Verse for Children.* 3rd ed. New York: The Macmillan Company, 1965.

HUUS, HELEN, ed. *Evaluating Books for Children and Young People.* Newark, Del.: International Reading Association, 1968.

INTERNATIONAL READING ASSOCIATION. *Children, Books and Reading.* Newark, Del.: International Reading Association, 1964.

217

JORDAN, ALICE M. *Children's Classics*. Boston: The Horn Book, 1960.

KINGMAN, LEE, ed. *Newbery and Caldecott Medal Books, 1956–1965*. Boston: The Horn Book, 1965.

KUNITZ, S. J., ed. *The Junior Book of Authors*. New York: The H. W. Wilson Company, 1951.

LADLEY, WINIFRED C., comp. *Sources of Good Books and Magazines for Children: An Annotated Bibliography*. Urbana: University of Illinois, 1965.

LARRICK, NANCY. *A Parent's Guide to Children's Reading*. Rev. ed. New York: Doubleday and Company, Inc., 1964.

LIBRARY ASSOCIATION. *Chosen for Children: An Account of the Books Which Have Been Awarded the Library Association Carnegie Medal, 1936–1957*. London, England: 1957.

THE LIBRARY JOURNAL. *Recommended Children's Books as Professionally Evaluated by Librarians for Librarians in the Junior Libraries Section of the Library Journal*. New York: 1951.

LINES, KATHLEEN. *Four to Fourteen: A Library of Books for Children*. 2nd ed. Cambridge, England: Published for the National Book League at the University Press, 1956.

LOCK, MURIEL. *Reference Material for Young People*. London, England: Bingley, 1967.

LOGASA, HANNAH. *Book Selection in Education for Children and Young Adults*. Boston: F. W. Faxon Co., Inc., 1965.

MARANTZ, KENNETH, comp. *A Bibliography of Children's Art Literature: An Annotated Bibliography of Children's Literature Designed to Stimulate and Enrich the Visual Imagination of the Child*. Washington, D. C.: National Art Association, 1965.

MEIGS, CORNELIA, *et al. Critical History of Children's Literature*. New York: The Macmillan Company, 1953.

METZNER, SEYMOUR. *American History in Juvenile Books: A Chrono-logical Guide.* New York: The H. W. Wilson Company, 1966.

MILLER, BERTHA E., ed. *Caldecott Medal Books, 1938–1957.* Boston: The Horn Book, 1957.
————, comp. *Illustrators of Children's Books, 1744–1945.* 1st ed. Boston: The Horn Book, 1947.
————. Supplement, 1946–1956.
————, ed. *Newbery Medal Books, 1922–1955.* Boston: The Horn Book, 1955.

MOORE, ANNE C. *My Roads to Childhood: Views and Reviews of Children's Books.* Boston: The Horn Book, 1961.

MUNSON, AMELIA. *An Ample Field.* Chicago: American Library Association, 1950.

NATIONAL ASSOCIATION OF INDEPENDENT SCHOOLS. *Junior Book List: Current Books.* Boston: 1964.

NATIONAL COUNCIL OF TEACHERS OF ENGLISH. Committee on the Elementary School Book List. *Adventures with Books: A Book List for Elementary Schools.* New York: New American Library, 1966.

NEW YORK LIBRARY ASSOCIATION. Children's and Young Adult Services Section. *Children's Book List for Small Public Libraries.* Albany: 1964.
————. *Recordings for Children.* 2nd ed., rev. New York: 1964.

NEW YORK PUBLIC LIBRARY. *Children's Books Suggested as Holiday Gifts.* New York: 1959.

PARKER, ELINOR M., comp. *Reading Is Fun: A Guide to Children's Literature.* New York: Charles Scribner's Sons, 1948.

PERKINS, RALPH. *Book Selection Media: A Descriptive Guide to 175 Aids for Selecting Library Materials.* Champaign, Ill.: National Council of Teachers of English, 1966.

PILGRIM, GENEVA H., AND MCALLISTER, MARIANA K. *Books, Young People and Reading Guidance.* 2nd ed. New York: Harper and Row Publishers, 1968.

PITTSBURGH, CARNEGIE LIBRARY. *Stories to Tell to Children: A Selected List for Use by Libraries, Schools, Clubs, and by Radio and Television Storytellers.* 7th ed. Pittsburgh: Carnegie Library of Pittsburgh, Boys and Girls Department, 1960.

PITZ, HENRY C. *Illustrating Children's Books.* New York: Watson-Guptill, 1963.

RAMSEY, ELOISE, comp. *Folklore for Children and Young People: A Critical Descriptive Bibliography for Use in the Elementary and Intermediate School.* Philadelphia, Pa.: American Folklore Society, 1952.

RASMUSSEN, MARGARET, ed. *Literature with Children.* Washington, D. C.: Association for Childhood Education, 1961.

*The Right Book for the Right Child: A Graded Buying List of Children's Books.* 3rd ed., rev. and reset. New York: The John Day Company, Inc., 1942.

ROOS, JEAN C. *What Shall We Read Next? A Program of Reading Sequences.* New York: The H. W. Wilson Company, 1940.

ROSENBACH, ABRAHAM S. W. *Early American Children's Books.* New York: Kraus Reprint Corp., 1966.

RUE, ELOISE. *Subject Index to Books for Intermediate Grades.* 2nd ed. Chicago: ALA, 1950.

SHEDLOCK, MARIE L. *The Art of the Storyteller.* 3rd ed., rev. With a new bibliography by Eulalie Steinmetz. New York: Dover Publishing Co., 1952.

SMITH, IRENE. *A History of the Newbery and Caldecott Medals.* New York: The Viking Press, Inc., 1957.

SPACHE, GEORGE D. *Good Reading for Poor Readers.* Rev. Champaign, Ill.: Garrard Publishing Company, 1966.

STRANG, RUTH M. *Gateways to Readable Books: An Annotated Grades List of Books in Many Fields for Adolescents Who Find Reading Difficult.* 4th ed. New York: The H. W. Wilson Company, 1966.

*Subject Index to Children's Magazines.* Edited by Meribah Hazen. Madison, Wis.: Library, Vol. 18, September 1965–August 1966.

TOOZE, RUTH. *Your Children Want to Read.* Englewood Cliffs, N. J.: Prentice-Hall, Inc., 1957.

TORONTO PUBLIC LIBRARIES. Boys and Girls Services. *Books for Boys and Girls.* 4th ed. Toronto, Canada: Ryerson Press, 1966.

U. S. CHILDREN'S BUREAU. Publication 304. *Children's Bookshelf: A Book List for Parents.* Rev. ed., 1953.

U. S. LIBRARY OF CONGRESS. *Children's Books, 1966: List of Books for Preschool through Junior High School Age.* Compiled by Virginia Haviland.
————. Reference Department. *Children's Literature: A Guide to Reference Sources.* Prepared under the direction of Virginia Haviland. Washington: Library of Congress, 1966.

VIGUERS, RUTH H. *Margin for Surprise: About Books, Children, and Libraries.* Boston: Little, Brown and Company, 1964.

VRIES, LEONARD DE, ed. *Flowers of Delight: Anthology Selected with the Greatest Care from Books for Juvenile Minds, 1765–1830.* New York: Pantheon Books, 1965.

WHITEHEAD, ROBERT. *Children's Literature: Strategies of Teaching.* Englewood Cliffs, N. J.: Prentice-Hall, Inc., 1968.

WILSON, H. W. FIRM, publishers. *Children's Catalog.* Edited by Rachel Shor and Estelle A. Fidell. 11th ed. New York: 1966.

# INDEX

*A Book of Children's Literature*, 108
*A Book of Moon Rockets for You*, 88
Activities, science, 91–92
Activities, social studies, 51
*Aesop's Fables*, 139
Affect of books, the, 140
*A Guide to Familiar American Insects*, 92
*A Guide to the Most Familiar American Birds*, 92
*Alice in Wonderland*, 200
*All About Our Changing Rocks*, 99
*All About Satellites and Space Ships*, 88
*A Long Way to Frisco*, 43
*Amos Fortune, Freeman*, 55
*...And Now Miguel*, 168
Andersen, Hans C., 167
*Anna Frank, A Portrait in Courage*, 56
Arbuthnot, May H., 108, 114
Ardizzone, Edward, 116
Armstrong, Neil, 40
Arts, the, 104
*A Teacher's Guide to Children's Books*, 108
*A Tree is a Plant*, 84
Award Winners, The, 191

Bacon, Francis, 138
Basal Readers, 6–15, 16–19, 23
*Batman*, 183
Beeler, Nelson F., 92
*Bible, The*, 137–138
Bibliotherapy, 158–162
*Biggest Bear, The*, 31
Billy the Kid, 128
Biography, 55–60, 89, 127
  kinds of, 55–56
*Biography of Andrew Jackson*, 56
*Black Tanker, The*, 168
*Bobbsey Twins, The*, 208
Bonham, Frank, 168
Book reports, 186
Book talks, 59, 110
Branley, Franklyn M., 87–88
*Br'er Rabbit*, 128
*Bright April*, 160
Brown, Marsha, 116, 172
Buffalo Bill, 128
*Building Bridges to Understanding*, 64
Bulla, Clyde R., 84
Bulletin boards, 59
*By the Shores of Silver Lake*, 212

223

*Call it Courage,* 31
Carlson, Natalie S., 160
Carlyle, Thomas, 138
*Challenge of the Universe,* 88
Chambers, Dewey, 125, 154–156
*Changing Face of North America, The,* 99
Chapbook, The, 182
*Charlotte's Web,* 31, 113, 114
Chase, Richard, 129
Chester, Michael, 43, 45, 88
*Children and Books,* 108
*Cinderella,* 129, 167
Classics, the, 200
  definition of, 200
  rewritten, 203
Coggins, Jack, 88
Columbus, 40
*Columbus Story, The,* 56
Commanger, Henry, 56
Conflicting evidence, 49, 93
Contemporary American fiction, 63
Controlled vocabulary, 29, 212
Cooper, Elizabeth K., 92
Cotton, John, 139
Craig, Gerald S., 91
Creative
  activity, 170
  drama, 123, 174
  drama, steps for, 125
  teaching, 18, 24, 165
  thinking, 166, 167
  writing, 110, 122, 171
Creativity, 105, 165
Criteria for cross reference, 93–94
Crosby, Muriel, 64, 65, 147, 148, 161
Cross reference checking, science, 93
*Crow Boy,* 160
Culturally disadvantaged, the, 26
Curriculum development, 25

Dalgliesh, Alice, 56
*Daniel Boone,* 55
Daugherty, James, 55
de Angeli, M., 160
Denys, Val Baker, 127
Development of taste in literature, 109
*Dick Whittington and His Cat,* 171
Didactic writing, 137
Dietz, David, 88
Disney, Walt, 169, 182, 204
Divergent thinking, 167
*Door in the Wall,* 160

Dramatic play, 170, 174
*Durango Street,* 168

*Earth for Sam, The,* 99
*Eclectic Reader, The,* 139
Emotional level in reading, 40, 44, 45
*Emperor's New Clothes, The,* 167
*Empty Schoolhouse, The,* 160
Ethnic groups, 16, 60–62, 64
Ethnocentrism, 60, 64, 145–146
*Experiments in Chemistry,* 92
*Experiments in the Principles of Space Travel,* 88
*Experiments with a Microscope,* 92
*Exploring by Astronaut, The Story of Project Mercury,* 88
*Eyes on the Ballet,* 127

*Fables of La Fontaine, The,* 139
Factual level in reading, 40, 41, 43, 52
*Familiar American Birds, A Guide to the Most,* 92
*Familiar Minerals, Gems, Ores and Rocks,* 99
Family chronicle, the, 211–212
Feeling, as a result of reading, 41, 45–46
*First Wagons to California,* 43, 45
Fitzgerald, Burdette, 125
Folk literature, 128–130
Frebold Freboldson, 128
*Frog Went A-Courtin',* 172
*Frontier Living,* 51

Gamow, George, 88
*George Patton, General in Spurs,* 56
*Globe for the Space Age, The,* 88
*Green Hornet, The,* 183
Growth in reading, as a result of literature, 10–15

Hannibal, 40
*Happy Golden Years, These,* 212
*Harvard Report on Reading in the Elementary School, The,* 21–22
Hatch, Alden, 56
Hawthorn, Hildegard, 43
Head Start Programs, 11
*Heidi,* 200–201
Hirsch, Carl, 88
Holling, Holling C., 43, 53, 54
Hollowell, Lillian, 108

Homze, Alma C., 153–154
Human relations, 60–65
Hynek, J. A., 88

Illustrations, 114–119, 167–170
Individualized reading, 19–23
Information gathering, 38, 84, 92, 99, 127
Informational books, 46–51, 84–85, 92, 99, 127
Intercultural, interracial fiction, 63
International fiction, 63
Island of the Blue Dolphins, 31, 169

Jack and the Beanstalk, 129
Jack Tales, The, 129
Joaquin Murietta, 128
John Henry, 128
Johnny Appleseed, 128
Johnston, Montgomery, 140
Judson, Clara, 56
Judy Bolton, 111
Jumping Frog of Calevaras County, The, 128
Jungle Book, The, 169
"Junk" literature, 111–114, 182

Keating, Charlotte M., 64
Kipling, R., 169
Krumgold, J., 168

Langstaff, John, 172
Language learning, 106–107
models, 107
Larrick, Nancy, 108
Lauber, Patricia, 99
Leisure time, 94–97
Lewis, Jerry, 183
Literary "junk", 111, 182–186
Little House in the Big Woods, The, 212
Little House on the Prairie, The, 212
Little Women, 200, 201
Loban, Walter, 147
Logan, Katherine, 138
Lowry, Heath, 156–158

McAuley, John D., 40
McClelland, David, 152–153
McClinton, David, 88
McFarland, Donald, 73–74

McGuffy, William H., 139
Macmillan Reading Spectrum, The, 206
Mafutu, 167
Manolo, 167
Mark Tidd, 208
Mary Poppins, 169
Meckel, Henry, 144, 148
Methods of teaching reading, 5–25
Michaelis, John, 41, 42, 43
Milk for Babes, Drawn Out of the Breasts of Both Testaments, 139
Moon, The, 88
Moon: Target for Apollo, The, 88
Mozart, The Wonder Boy, 127
Munari, Bruno, 114
Munch, Theodore, 88
Mural painting, 174
Murals, 52–54

Nancy Drew, 111–114, 208
National Science Foundation, The, 86
Newbery awards, 111, 156
winners, 111
New England Primer, The, 139
Nicholas, 172

O'Dell, Scott, 169
On the Banks of Plum Creek, 212
Oral tradition, the, 128–130
Oral reading, 59, 106–108, 110

Paperbacks, the, 205
Paperbound Book Guide for Elementary Schools, 207
Paperbound Books in Print, 207
Paul Bunyan, 128
Pease, Howard, 8, 168
Pecos Bill, 128
Peter Rabbit, 172, 200
Philobiblon, 138
Philosophy of reading, 4–6
Piatti, Celestino, 116
Picture books, 53–54, 114
Piltz, Albert, 74
Play making, 123–127
Play with Seeds, 84
Playwright, 122
Poetry, 119, 170, 172
Poetry, introduction to, 119
Poetry, writing, 121–122
Politi, Leo, 56
Potter, Beatrix, 172

*Potter, The Young,* 127
Powers, Alfred, 43
Pratt, Fletcher, 88
Priestly, J. B., 127
Psycological level, 107
*Puss in Boots,* 172

Ragan, William, 40
Reading
  growth with literature, 10–15
  at home, 9
  individualized, 19–23
  methods of teaching, 4–30
  philosophy of, 4–6
  reason for teaching, 6–30
  remedial reader, 25–29
  research in, 4–5
  self-selection, 19–23
  skills of, 10–15
*Reading Ladders for Human Relations,*
  65, 147, 161
Realistic fiction, 63
Recordings, 121
Reed, W. M., 99
Regional literature, 61, 63
Reid, Virginia, 147
Research, by children, 46, 47
*Rip Van Winkle,* 128
*Robert E. Lee,* 56
*Robin Hood,* 200
*Robinson Crusoe,* 200
*Rockets, Satellites, and Space Travel,* 88
*Rocks and Minerals, A Guide To,* 99
Rogers, Roy, 182
Rojankovsky, Teodor, 172
*Rumplestiltskin,* 167
Russell, David, 143–144, 148–150

*St. Francis and the Animals,* 56
Sales, Soupy, 182
Schnabel, Ernst, 56
Schulberg, Budd, 138
Science
  activity, 91–93
  enrichment, 88–92
  hobby, 94–99
  lesson, 81–85
  new development in, 78–81
  process of, 74–76
  textbook, 76–81, 88
*Science in Your Own Backyard,* 92
*Seeds and More Seeds,* 84
Self-selection, reading plan, 19–23

Selsam, Millicent, 84
Sendak, Maurice, 116
Series, The, 112, 208
Shakespeare, 120, 167
Shepard, John, 150–152
Skills, reading, 10–15, 15–19
Smith, James A., 116
Social studies
  activities with, 51–54
  conflicting evidence, 49
  definition of, 40
  emotional dimension, 44–46
  factual level, 44–46
  feeling with, 44
  information gathering for, 46–54
  informational book in, 46–51
  research in, 46–54
  textbooks, 41–43
Space, 87–88
Stefferud, Alfred, 84
Stillman, Nathan, 74
Strickland, Ruth, 141
*Stuart Little,* 113
*Sue Barton,* 208
*Sweet Betsy from Pike,* 128
*Swiss Family Robinson,* 200, 204
Symbolic level, 107
Syrocki, John, 99

Taba, Hilda, 64, 65, 144–147
Talent, 105
Taste, development of, 109–112
Television, 122
Temple, Shirley, 182
*Theatre, The Wonderful World of,* 127
*Toad of Toad Hall,* 167
*Tom Sawyer,* 31, 167, 168, 200, 201
Tom Swift, 112
*Treasure Island,* 200
*Tree in the Trail,* 43, 53, 54
Tunis, Edwin, 51
Twain, Mark, 168
*Two Reds, The,* 172

Understanding others, 60–65, 142–150,
  158–162

Values in literature, 137, 141, 150–158

Walker, Katherine, 127
Waples, Douglas, 142, 143

Ward, Lynd, 116
Weber, Olga, 207
Wheeler, Opal, 127
*Wheels Toward the West*, 43
White, E. B., 113
Wilder, Laura I., 212
Will, 172
Williams, Garth, 114
*With Perspective on Human Relations:*

*A Study of Peer Group Dynamics in an Eighth Grade*, 64
*Wonders of Seeds*, 84

Yates, Elizabeth, 55

Zim, Harold, 92, 99

PRINTED IN U.S.A.